ANTI-INFLAMMATORY DIET COOKBOOK FOR BEGINNERS

A Quick Guide for the Anti-inflammatory Diet with Easy and Tasty Recipes that the family will love. Balance hormones and heal the Immune system with a meal plan included.

D1710317

Olivia J. Fisher

Table of Contents

Introduction

This book will teach you how to eat healthily in order to avoid chronic inflammation. This book has selected the best items from the list and presented them to you for inclusion in your diet. It discusses the benefits of eating a healthy anti-inflammatory diet.

Anti-inflammatory eating is a way of life. This meal plan includes eating foods high in antioxidants, omega-3 fatty acids, and fiber on a daily basis. Many studies confirm that the anti-inflammatory diet is a true health ally. It is capable of reducing or eliminating inflammations that favor chronic diseases such as arthritis, gastritis, Crohn's disease, ulcerative colitis in the most severe cases and premature aging, general malaise, cardiovascular aging, and much more in the mildest cases if followed consistently over time.

Adopting an anti-inflammatory diet can help you stay healthy and fully enjoy life's gifts. It is critical to remember that a lack of time is merely an excuse we use to avoid doing something. We can devote all of our time to ourselves if we so desire.

An anti-inflammatory diet will improve your quality of life. You'll feel rejuvenated, healthy, and renewed. You wouldn't experience the guilt that comes with eating the wrong food. You will be able to easily manage your weight. You will also be able to avoid unwanted medical issues if you follow a good anti-inflammatory diet.

All you have to do is make a choice and eat the right foods. Your immune system is activated when your body recognizes something foreign, such as an invading bacterium, plant pollen, or a chemical. As a result, inflammation increases.

There are numerous health benefits to eating an anti-inflammatory diet. Some serious diseases, such as heart disease, obesity, and even rheumatoid arthritis, are thought to be caused by inflammation. The term "environmental stewardship" refers to the process of protecting the environment through the use of stewardship.

When you're fighting inflammation, you know you're in a fight. There is always so much going on in your body and mind that it can be exhausting and overwhelming. Fatigue is, after all, a symptom of inflammation for a reason!

The purpose of this book is to provide you with practical and simple resources to assist you in preparing wholesome and nourishing meals on a daily basis. You won't have to spend any extra money, energy, or time learning about the anti-inflammatory diet. A healthy meal plan is within your grasp and can mean the difference between living a healthy life and becoming ill. Nutrition is critical in treating all types of inflammation.

You must understand that the anti-inflammatory diet is intended to aid in internal healing. It is about consuming foods that will help your body heal itself, not about going on an extreme diet.

An anti-inflammatory diet is just as beneficial as a diet for weight loss or heart health. It will help reduce inflammation if you have successfully maintained your immune system. It will not only help you avoid autoimmune disorders, but it will also aid in the treatment of diabetes, heart disease, and Alzheimer's disease.

A healthy diet must include a variety of plant-based foods like fruits and vegetables, complex carbohydrates like whole-grain bread and pasta, and a moderate amount of dairy products and red meat.

So here I am, writing this book to disseminate information about chronic inflammation in the hopes that people will understand that what they put into their bodies matters. What you eat has a direct impact on your well-being — right down to the cellular level. Of course, you'll find some of my favorite delectable recipes to get you started!

Let's get started.

What Anti-Inflammatory Diet Is All About

Chronic inflammation in the human body can lead to serious diseases like Alzheimer's, cancer, rheumatoid arthritis, and heart disease. Inflammation is typically the body's response to an infection or injury. Inflammation causes swelling, redness, and discomfort. However, if it lasts longer or occurs for no apparent reason, it is a sign that the body is being harmed. Smoking, stressful work, a lack of exercise, and eating unhealthy foods can all contribute to chronic inflammation.

To avoid becoming seriously ill and fighting inflammation, a patient must follow an anti-inflammatory diet. The diet plan can help prevent illnesses as well as aid in weight loss. This aids in the maintenance of a patient's health.

An anti-inflammatory diet should include a daily intake of 2,000–3,000 calories, 67 g of fat, and 2,300 mg of sodium. Fifty percent (50%) of these calories are expected to come from carbohydrates, twenty percent (20%) from protein, and thirty percent (30%) from fat.

Whole-wheat grains, sweet potatoes, squash, bulgur wheat, beans, and brown rice are all high in carbohydrates.

Your fat intake, on the other hand, will come from most types of fish and any foods cooked in extra-virgin olive oil or organic canola oil. Protein can be obtained from soybeans and other products containing whole soy.

This diet forbids the consumption of fast food or processed foods in any form. It entails limiting the consumption of pork, beef, sugar, milk, and margarine. For people with heart problems, an anti-inflammatory diet should also include less processed diabetic sugar and low cholesterol (though Omega-3 is a good cholesterol found in a variety of fish).

One of the benefits of an anti-inflammatory diet is that it incorporates new, phytonutrient-rich foods that avoid degenerative diseases. The addition of Omega-3 fatty acids to the diet plan also provides cardiovascular benefits. These fatty acids help to prevent heart problems and lower "bad" cholesterol and blood pressure levels.

Another advantage of the anti-inflammatory diet is that it can help diabetics. This diet is ideal for diabetic patients because it eliminates processed sugar as well as sugary meals and snacks. Although the diet does not significantly reduce weight, it does reduce the likelihood of an individual developing obesity. This is due to the inclusion of natural fruits and vegetables while excluding meat and other processed foods.

By lowering the level of inflammation in the body, an anti-inflammatory diet can help to reduce the risk of these conditions.

The Anti-inflammatory diet is designed to help people suffering from chronic inflammation. The book contains recipes that use ingredients known to help reduce inflammation and information on which foods to avoid. The recipes in the book are categorized by type of food, so people can easily find the right recipe for their needs. In addition, the book includes tips on how to make the recipes more accessible for people with different dietary requirements. For example, many of the recipes can be made gluten-free or lactose-free. The Anti-inflammatory Cookbook is a valuable resource for anyone looking to reduce their inflammation levels.

What is Meal planning

Simply put, meal planning is the process of preparing and storing several individual servings of one or more weekly meals and snacks ahead of time. Meal planning goes beyond selecting and scheduling meals by having them fully cooked and boxed. Depending on your needs and schedule, meal planning can be done 1 or 2 days per week. The same meal will be divided and boxed for several meals throughout the week and will be ready to heat and eat, similar to a casserole, or eat cold, similar to a salad. However, the advantages of meal planning extend far beyond mere convenience.

Why should you plan your meals?

Meal planning is the single most important reason I can feed myself and my family healthy, delicious meals every day. Meal planning has the following advantages:

- Saving money: If you know what you're going to cook, you can plan ahead of time. Meat and other ingredients can be purchased in bulk, divided into meal portions, and stored in resealable plastic bags in the refrigerator or freezer. This allows you to stretch your food budget.

- Time savings: Although you will spend some time in the kitchen on a specific day of your choosing, you will not be slaving over a hot stove for hours during the week. Plus, you won't have much cleaning to do on those hectic weeknights. Instead, use those extra 30 to 60 minutes to spend quality time with loved ones!

- Controlling portions: To make a meal last, divide the food and keep track of the portions. To make your life easier, each of my recipes includes precise portion measurements. Controlling portions not only saves money but also keeps meal and snack calories under control.

- Making more progress with less effort: Some nights, it feels like you're cooking nonstop while your to-do list grows and grows. Preparing a double batch of chili or burgers ahead of time requires less effort than cooking a new meal every night; even on busy weeknights, you'll be able to sit down, breathe, and enjoy a healthy meal.

- Eating more healthily: A quick stop at a fast-food restaurant or a visit to the vending machine will be a thing of the past. Many high-calorie, high-fat, and high-sugar foods are consumed in these unhealthy settings. These unhealthy eating habits begin to fade when you are armed with prepared meals and snacks.

- Improving Multitasking Capabilities: Meal planning will hone and even improve your multitasking abilities. You'll learn how to set an oven timer while making the dressing for your lunch salad. You can save time and become more efficient at meal planning if you multitask.

Meal plan Principles

Developing good meal-planning habits is an important part of the learning process. Here are some meal planning dos and don'ts to remember as you get started:

1. DO mark healthy recipes that you enjoy. After experimenting with healthy recipes, save your favorites in a folder or mark them in a cookbook.

2. DO proceed at your own pace. You can meal plan successfully with 3 or 6 recipes. You don't have to make ten or more recipes for the week. Begin slowly and work your way up.

3. DO work around your schedule. You'll be able to prepare more recipes in some weeks than others. Do whatever is most convenient for you and your schedule.

4. DO keep any leftovers in the freezer. You will have a few extra meals some weeks. Freezer-friendly meals can be frozen and stored for several months as specified in the recipes.

5. DO make cleanup simple. You'll have a lot of vegetable scraps, eggshells, and empty containers to dispose of, so keep your recycling bin, compost bin, and trash can close by for easy cleanup.

6. DON'T put things off until the last minute. Plan ahead of time for the best results. Meal planning entails planning your time ahead of time so that you can go to the market and buy the ingredients you need, then spend the time necessary at home preparing them.

7. DO NOT SEPARATE MEALS LATER. The final step in meal planning is to portion out recipes and pack them into containers. Do not skip this step or divide meals right before eating. Meal preparation aids in portion control, eliminates last-minute meal prep, and ensures that your meals will last the entire week.

8. DO NOT OVERPREPARE. The last thing you want to do is prepare meals that will go uneaten unless they can be frozen. Start slowly and get to know your Meal planning needs to get into the Meal planning groove. You can meal plan one or two days per week, depending on your schedule.

Getting Started with Meal Preparation

There are simple steps you can take to ensure meal-planning success. Planning ahead for your prep days, grocery shopping, and efficiently preparing and packaging your meals will save you time in the long run.

1. Select your prep day (s). It doesn't matter which day you choose to meal plan, but you'll need about 4 hours to cook your recipes and divide them into their weekly containers.
   This book's plans are intended to last 5 days. For example, you could prepare meals for Monday through Friday on Sunday. If you have a different schedule, modify the plan to meet your requirements.

2. Make a strategy. The first 6 weeks of meal-prep plans are already planned for you. Following that, you'll be able to plan your own meals or substitute recipes into the existing structure. Set aside 30 minutes to an hour each week to make your plan, and consider doing it a day or two before your prep day to allow for grocery shopping. Make use of the prep charts in this book as a model.

3. Go shopping for groceries. Make a shopping list once you've decided on a strategy. To save time while shopping, organize your ingredients by aisle, such as bulk, herbs and spices, dry goods, refrigerated items, fresh produce, frozen foods, and so on.

4. Prepare and cook the food. Take out the ingredients and kitchen tools you'll need for each recipe before you begin cooking. Make a cooking plan once everything is in place. Examine the timing of the recipes and decide which one to prepare first. It will become easier as you practice. For example, while a sheet pan meal is roasting, you can prepare a sauce. You can chop similar ingredients all at once; for example, if 3 recipes call for parsley, chop the entire amount at once and portion it out accordingly.

5. Separate and pack. Once your meals are ready, go over the weekly plan and serving sizes, and place all of your containers on the counter. Portion the meals into their containers according to the meal plan's serving size.

    Label and date as needed, and keep them visible in the refrigerator or freezer.

6. Snap and go. Consider purchasing a thermal lunch bag and reusable utensils for on-the-go breakfast or lunch. Meal planning is useless if you forget to bring your food!

Chapter #1: Ingredients: Food to Consume or to Avoid

Foods to eat

To combat inflammation, eat a diet rich in anti-inflammatory foods.

Inflammation-fighting foods include:

- Salmon and tuna are examples of oily fish.
- Strawberries, blueberries, cherries, and blackberries are examples of fruits.
- Broccoli, kale, and spinach are examples of vegetables.
- Fiber
- Beans
- Nuts and seeds
- Olives and olive oil
- Cooked or moderately cooked vegetables
- Lentils and other legumes
- Herbs and spices such as turmeric and ginger
- Prebiotics and probiotics are both beneficial bacteria.
- Tea
- Kale and spinach are examples of dark leafy greens.
- Grapes
- Broccoli and cauliflower
- Tea made from grass
- Lentils and beans
- Avocado and coconut
- Olives
- Extra-virgin olive oil
- Walnuts, almonds, pistachios, pine nuts, and other nuts

- Cold water fish (as well as other types of fish) such as salmon and sardines
- Spices such as cinnamon, turmeric, and others
- Chocolate
- Eggs from Watermelon
- Tomatoes

It's important to remember that not one meal can make someone's health better. It's crucial to eat a variety of healthy meals.

The best ingredients are created using just pure, natural substances. During processing, food may lose part of its nutritious content.

Consumers should carefully read the labels on prepared foods. However, even though cocoa is a fantastic alternative, it typically includes sugar and fat. A colorful dish may include many of the minerals and antioxidants in cocoa. You should incorporate colorful fruits and vegetables into your diet.

Foods to Avoid

People who are following an anti-inflammatory diet should avoid or eat the following as little as possible:

- Processed foods
- Foods including added salt or sugar
- Unhealthful oils
- Processed carbs that are present in white pasta, white bread, and a variety of baked goods
- Processed snack meals, including crackers chips
- Premade desserts, including ice cream cookies, and candy
- Excess alcohol

People may also find it beneficial to decrease their consumption of the following:

Gluten: Some people get an inflammatory reaction after consuming gluten. A gluten-free diet has benefits and drawbacks, but it's not for everyone. It may be possible to reduce a person's symptoms by eliminating gluten for a while before deciding if it is beneficial.

Nightshades: Eating nightshade vegetables, including potatoes, peppers, tomatoes, and eggplants, may cause flare-ups in particular people with inflammatory diseases. There isn't much evidence to back up this assertion, but one might try cutting out nightshades from their diet for two to three weeks to see if their symptoms improve.

Carbohydrates: Several pieces of data indicate that a high-carb diet may cause inflammation in certain people even when the carbs are healthy for you. Despite high carbohydrate content, foods like sweet potatoes and whole grains are rich sources of antioxidants and nutrients.

Red Meat: It is a major source of inflammation in the body. It is known to increase 3 blood markers associated with heart disease and cancer. Homocysteine, C-reactive protein (CRP), and lipoprotein are examples of these.

Trans Fat: They are linked to an increased risk of heart disease, stroke, diabetes, and inflammatory diseases such as Crohn's and rheumatoid arthritis.

Whole Milk: According to a study published in Nutrition Research, drinking whole milk can cause inflammation in overweight adults.

When exposed to sugar, the body can produce more inflammatory proteins. This increase has been linked to a variety of health problems, including asthma, rheumatoid arthritis, and Alzheimer's disease.

Some Artificial Food Coloring (AFC) have been approvals in US such us Blue #1 and #2, common called Brillant Blue and Indigotine. These dyes are frequently used in food products to make them appear more vibrant and appealing, but they have been linked to an increased risk of allergies, cancer, ADHD, and inflammation.

Caffeine is a natural stimulant that acts on your brain to improve memory, mood, reaction times and mental function, but an excessive dose can cause dehydration, interfere with a good night's sleep and has negative impact linked elevated blood pressure.

Chapter #2: Breakfast

1. Spiced Oatmeal

Preparation Time: 10 minutes

Cooking Time: 3 minutes

Servings: 2

Ingredients:

- 2/3 cup unsweetened coconut milk
- ½ cup gluten-free quick-cooking oats
- 1 organic egg white
- ½ tsp ground turmeric
- ½ tsp ground cinnamon
- ¼ tsp ground ginger

Directions:

1. In a microwave-safe bowl, blend together milk and oats, and microwave on a High setting for about 1 minute.
2. Remove from the microwave and stir in the egg white until well blended.
3. Add in the spices and stir until well blended.
4. Microwave on a High setting for about 2 minutes, stirring after every 20 seconds.
5. Serve warm with your favorite topping.

Nutrition:

Nutritional Info (per serving)				
Calories	*Fat*	*Carbs*	*Fiber*	*Protein*
659	16 g	57 g	3 g	12 g

2. Quinoa and Pumpkin

Preparation Time: 10 minutes

Cooking Time: 17 minutes

Servings: 6

Ingredients:

- 3 ½ cups filtered water
- 1 ¾ cup quinoa, soaked for 15 minutes and rinsed
- 16 oz unsweetened coconut milk
- 1 ¾ cup sugar-free pumpkin puree
- 2 tsp ground cinnamon
- 1 tsp ground ginger
- Pinch ground cloves
- Pinch ground nutmeg
- Salt, as required
- 3 Tbsp extra-virgin coconut oil
- 4–6 drops liquid stevia
- 1 tsp organic vanilla extract

Directions:

1. In a saucepan, add the water and quinoa over high heat.
2. Cover the pan and bring to a boil.
3. Reduce the heat to low and simmer for about 12 minutes or until all the liquid is absorbed.
4. Add the remaining ingredients and stir until well combined.
5. Immediately remove from the heat and serve warm.

Nutrition:

Nutritional Info (per serving)				
Calories	Fat	Carbs	Fiber	Protein
743	23 g	98 g	6.3 g	12 g

3. Banana Pancakes

Preparation Time: 10 minutes

Cooking Time: 10 minutes

Servings: 2

Ingredients:

- ¼ cup arrowroot flour
- ¼ cup gluten-free rolled oats
- ½ tsp organic baking powder
- ¼ tsp baking soda
- ⅛ tsp ground cinnamon
- ¼ cup unsweetened almond milk
- 2 organic egg whites
- 2 tsp coconut oil, softened and divided
- ½ banana, peeled and mashed
- ⅛ tsp organic vanilla extract

Directions:

1. Place the oats, flour, baking powder, baking soda and cinnamon in a large-sized bowl, and mix well.
2. In another bowl, add the milk, egg whites, 1 tsp of coconut oil, banana and vanilla extract, and beat until well combined.
3. Add the egg mixture to the flour mixture and mix until well combined.
4. Grease a large-sized frying pan with the remaining coconut oil and heat over low heat.
5. Add half of the mixture and cook for about 1–2 minutes per side.
6. Repeat with the remaining mixture and serve warm

Nutition:

Nutritional Info (per serving)				
Calories	*Fat*	*Carbs*	*Fiber*	*Protein*
1248	38 g	126 g	2.5 g	37 g

4. Cauliflower and Kale Bowl with Avocado

Preparation Time: 5 minutes

Cooking Time: 5 minutes

Servings: 1

Ingredients:

- 1 tsp extra-virgin olive oil
- 4 kale leaves, thoroughly washed and chopped
- 1 ½ cup cauliflower florets
- ½ avocado, chopped
- 1 tsp freshly squeezed lemon juice
- Pinch salt

Directions:

1. Pour 2 inches of water into a medium pot and insert a steamer basket. Bring to a boil over high heat.
2. Place the kale and cauliflower into the basket. Cover and steam for 5 minutes.
3. In a medium bowl, place the steamed vegetables. Add the avocado, lemon juice, olive oil and salt, and toss them well.

Nutrition:

Nutritional Info (per serving)				
Calories	*Fat*	*Carbs*	*Fiber*	*Protein*
327	6 g	124 g	0 g	8 g

5. Chia Seed Pudding with cherries on Top

Preparation Time: 10 minutes

Cooking Time: 15 minutes

Servings: 4

Ingredients:

- ½ cup chia seeds
- 2 cups unsweetened almond milk
- 1 tsp vanilla extract
- ¼ cup maple syrup or raw honey
- 1 cup frozen no-added-sugar pitted cherries, thawed, juice reserved, divided
- ½ cup chopped cashews, divided

Directions:

1. Add the chia seeds, almond milk, vanilla and maple syrup to a quart jar with a tight-fitting lid. Shake well and set aside for at least 15 minutes, or refrigerate overnight.
2. Evenly divide the pudding among 4 bowls and top with ¼ cup of cherries and 2 Tbsp of cashews in each bowl. Serve.

Nutrition:

Nutritional Info (per serving)				
Calories	*Fat*	*Carbs*	*Fiber*	*Protein*
972	34 g	188 g	0 g	21 g

6. Chickpea Fritters

Preparation Time: 15 minutes

Cooking Time: 20 minutes

Servings: 6

Ingredients:

- 1 Tbsp coconut oil, or extra-virgin olive oil
- 2 cups chickpea flour
- 2 Tbsp chia seeds, ground
- ½ tsp salt
- 3 cups lightly packed spinach leaves, finely chopped
- 1 ½ cup water

Directions:

Add the chickpea flour, water, chia seeds and salt to a medium bowl, mixing well to ensure there are no lumps.

1. Fold in the spinach.
2. Add the coconut oil to a nonstick skillet. Heat over medium-low heat.
3. Drop the batter into the pan with a ¼-cup measure. Flatten the fritters to about ½ inch thick. Don't crowd the pan. Working in batches.
4. Cook for 5 to 6 minutes. Flip the fritters and cook for another 5 minutes.
5. After all the batter has been cooked, transfer the fritters to a serving plate and serve hot.

Nutrition:

Nutritional Info (per serving)				
Calories	Fat	Carbs	Fiber	Protein
436	10 g	75 g	0 g	12 g

7. Banana Baked Oatmeal

Preparation Time: 5 minutes

Cooking Time: 7 minutes

Servings: 6

Ingredients:

- 3 cups oats
- ¼ tsp salt
- 2 bananas
- 2 eggs
- ⅓ cup xylitol

Directions:

1. Mix the oats, salt, bananas, eggs and xylitol in a medium bowl. Lightly spray a cake pan.
2. Add the oat mixture to the pan. Place 11 cups of water into the inner pot. Put a steam rack in the inner pot and the pan on it. Fix the lid.
3. Set the timer to 7 minutes on the Manual or Pressure Cook button.
4. Quickly remove pressure until the float valve drops, then unlock the lid. Wait 5 minutes before serving the porridge.

Nutrition:

Nutritional Info (per serving)				
Calories	*Fat*	*Carbs*	*Sodium*	*Protein*
921	35 g	79 g	186 mg	65 g

8. Banana Walnut Steel-Cut Oats

Preparation Time: 2 minutes

Cooking Time: 4 minutes

Servings: 4

Ingredients:

- 2 cups oats
- 2 ½ cups water
- 2 ½ cups vanilla almond milk
- 3 bananas
- 1 ½ tsp cinnamon
- 1 tsp vanilla extract
- ¼ tsp salt
- 4 Tbsp walnut pieces

Directions:

1. Stir in the steel-cut oats, the other ingredients and salt. Fix the lid.
2. Set the Instant Pot to Pressure Cook for 4 minutes. After 15 minutes, quick-release any leftover pressure until the float valve lowers, then open the lid.
3. Each plate of oats is topped with 1 Tbsp of chopped walnuts.

Nutrition:

Nutritional Info (per serving)				
Calories	*Fat*	*Carbs*	*Sodium*	*Protein*
1127	9 g	232 g	156 mg	16 g

9. Spinach and Artichoke Egg Casserole

Preparation Time: 10 minutes

Cooking Time: 18 minutes

Servings: 8

Ingredients:

- 10 eggs
- ¼ cup water
- 4 cups spinach
- 1 can baby artichoke
- 1 Tbsp chives
- 1 Tbsp lemon juice

Directions:

1. Spray cooking spray in a round glass bowl.
2. Whisk the eggs and water in a medium bowl, then add the spinach, artichokes, chives and lemon juice.
3. Pour the mixture into the pan. In the inner pot, add 2 cups of water and the steam rack.
4. Set the pan on the steam rack. Fix the lid. Set the timer to 18 minutes.
5. Quickly remove pressure until the float valve drops, then unlock the lid.
6. Allow it cool for 5 minutes before slicing and serving.

Nutrition:

Nutritional Info (per serving)				
Calories	Fat	Carbs	Sodium	Protein
2787	136 g	115 g	176 mg	155 g

10.   Coconut Almond Granola

Preparation Time: 5 minutes

Cooking Time: 7 minutes

Servings: 8

Ingredients:

- 1 ½ cup rolled oats
- ½ cup unsweetened shredded coconut
- ¼ cup monk fruit sweetener
- ⅛ tsp salt
- ¾ cup almond butter
- ¼ cup coconut oil

Directions:

1. Mix oats, coconut, sweetener and salt in a medium bowl. Mix in the almond butter and oil.
2. Prepare a cake pan with nonstick spray. Add the oat mixture to the pan and 1 cup of water to the Instant Pot inner pot.
3. Place the steam rack inside and the pan on top. Fix the lid. Set the timer to 7 minutes on the Manual or Pressure Cook button.
4. Quickly remove pressure until the float valve drops, then unlock the lid.
5. Remove the pan from the inner pot and cool thoroughly before serving.

Nutrition:

Nutritional Info (per serving)				
Calories	*Fat*	*Carbs*	*Sodium*	*Protein*
689	9 g	146 g	126 mg	12 g

11.   Easy Coconut Pancakes

Preparation Time: 10 minutes

Cooking Time: about 5 minutes per pancake

Servings: 4

Ingredients:

- 1 cup (240 ml) unsweetened coconut milk, plus additional as needed
- ½ cup (240 ml) coconut flour
- 4 organic eggs
- 1 Tbsp melted coconut oil, plus additional for greasing the pan
- 1 Tbsp maple syrup
- 1 tsp vanilla extract
- 1 tsp baking soda
- ½ tsp salt

Directions:

1. Mix the coconut milk, eggs, maple syrup, coconut oil and vanilla in a medium bowl with an electric mixer.
2. Stir the baking soda, coconut flour and salt in a small bowl. Add these dry ingredients to the wet ingredients and combine well until smooth and lump free.
3. If the batter is too thick, add additional liquid to dilute to the consistency of the pancake batter.
4. Lightly grease a large skillet with coconut oil. Put it over medium-high heat.
5. Add the batter in ½-cup scoops and cook for about 3 minutes until golden brown. Flip and cook for another 2 minutes.
6. Stack the pancakes on a plate while cooking the remaining batter. This makes about 8 pancakes.

Nutrition:

Nutritional Info (per serving)				
Calories	*Fat*	*Carbs*	*Fiber*	*Protein*
1348	65 g	98 g	6 g	63 g

12.   Easy Overnight Oats

Preparation Time: 10 minutes

Cooking Time: 0

Servings: 2

Ingredients:

- 1 ¾ cup unsweetened almond milk
- 1 cup oats (certified gluten-free if necessary)
- 2 Tbsp maple syrup
- ¼ tsp vanilla extract
- 1 Tbsp chia seeds (optional)

Optional Toppings:

- ¼ cup coconut oil
- 1 cup mixed berries
- ½ cup Greek yogurt
- 1 Tbsp toasted almonds
- 1 Tbsp toasted coconut

Directions:

1. In a jar with a tight-fitting lid, add the milk, oats, maple syrup, vanilla and chia seeds (if using), shaking well.
2. Place in the refrigerator and chill overnight.
3. Chill until it's ready to serve, divide the mixture between 2 serving bowls, top with your choices, and serve.

Nutrition:

Nutritional Info (per serving)				
Calories	*Fat*	*Carbs*	*Fiber*	*Protein*
1269	**23 g**	**80 g**	**0 g**	**19 g**

13.   Carrots Breakfast Mix

Preparation Time: 10 minutes

Cooking Time: 0 minutes

Servings: 4

Ingredients:

- 1 ½ Tbsp maple syrup
- 1 tsp olive oil
- 1 Tbsp chopped walnuts
- 1 onion, chopped
- 4 cups shredded carrots
- 1 Tbsp curry powder
- ¼ tsp ground turmeric
- Black pepper, to taste
- 2 Tbsp sesame seed paste
- ¼ cup lemon juice
- ½ cup chopped parsley

Directions:

1. In a salad bowl, mix the onion with the carrots, turmeric, curry powder, black pepper, lemon juice and parsley.
2. Add the maple syrup, oil, walnuts and sesame seed paste.
3. Toss well and serve for breakfast.
4. Enjoy!

Nutrition:

Nutritional Info (per serving)				
Calories	*Fat*	*Carbs*	*Fiber*	*Protein*
257	5 g	21 g	12 g	8 g

14. Italian Breakfast Salad

Preparation Time: 10 minutes

Cooking Time: 0 minutes

Servings: 4

Ingredients:

- 1 handful kalamata olives, pitted and sliced
- 1 cup cherry tomatoes, halved
- 1 ½ cucumbers, sliced
- 1 red onion, chopped
- 2 Tbsp chopped oregano
- 1 Tbsp chopped mint

For the Salad Dressing:

- 2 Tbsp balsamic vinegar
- ¼ cup olive oil
- 1 garlic clove, minced
- 2 tsp dried Italian herbs
- A pinch salt and black pepper

Directions:

1. In a salad bowl, toss together the olives with the tomatoes, cucumbers, onion, mint and oregano.
2. In a smaller bowl, whisk the vinegar with the oil, garlic, Italian herbs, salt and pepper.
3. Pour the dressing over the salad, toss, and serve for breakfast.
4. Enjoy!

Nutrition:

Calories	Fat	Carbs	Fiber	Protein
297	10 g	43 g	23 g	3 g

Nutritional Info (per serving)

15.   Zucchini and Sprout Breakfast Mix

Preparation Time: 10 minutes

Cooking Time: 0 minutes

Servings: 4

Ingredients:

- 2 zucchinis, spiralized
- 2 cups bean sprouts
- 4 green onions, chopped
- 1 red bell pepper, chopped
- Juice 1 lime
- 1 Tbsp olive oil
- ½ cup chopped cilantro
- ¾ cup almonds chopped
- A pinch salt and black pepper

Directions:

1. In a salad bowl, toss together the zucchini with the bean sprouts, green onions, bell pepper, cilantro, almonds, salt, pepper, lime juice and oil.
2. Serve for breakfast.

Nutrition:

Nutritional Info (per serving)				
Calories	*Fat*	*Carbs*	*Fiber*	*Protein*
967	**9 g**	**127 g**	**12 g**	**27 g**

16.   Breakfast Corn Salad

Preparation Time: 10 minutes

Cooking Time: 0 minutes

Servings: 4

Ingredients:

- 2 avocados, pitted, peeled and cubed
- 1 pint mixed cherry tomatoes, halved
- 2 cups fresh corn kernels
- 1 red onion, chopped

For the Salad Dressing:

- 2 Tbsp olive oil
- 1 Tbsp lime juice
- ½ tsp grated lime zest
- A pinch salt and black pepper
- ¼ cup chopped cilantro

Directions:

1. In a salad bowl, mix the avocados with the tomatoes, corn and onion. Add the oil, lime juice, lime zest, salt, pepper and cilantro, toss and serve for breakfast.

Nutrition:

Nutritional Info (per serving)				
Calories	Fat	Carbs	Fiber	Protein
876	36 g	57 g	2 g	12 g

17.   Cilantro Pancakes

Preparation Time: 10 minutes

Cooking Time: 6–8 minutes

Servings: 6

Ingredients:

- 1 cup coconut milk
- ½ cup tapioca flour
- ½ tsp powdered chili
- ¼ tsp turmeric, ground
- ½ (red) onion, chopped
- ½ cup almond flour
- Black pepper, freshly ground, to taste
- 1 (½-inch) ginger, grated finely
- ½ cup cilantro, chopped fresh
- 1 Serrano pepper, minced
- Salt, to taste
- Oil, as needed

Directions:

1. The flour and spices should be combined in a large mixing basin.
2. Coconut milk should be added and thoroughly mixed up.
3. Combine the ginger, onion, Serrano pepper and cilantro in a mixing bowl.
4. A large nonstick pan should be lightly oiled and heated over medium-low heat.
5. The batter should be added in a 14-cup volume, and then the pan should be turned to distribute the batter uniformly.
6. Cooking takes 3 to 4 minutes per side.
7. The leftover mixture should be used again.Serve with your preferred garnishes

Nutrition:

Nutritional Info (per serving)				
Calories	*Fat*	*Carbs*	*Fiber*	*Protein*
596	28 g	48 g	0 g	25 g

18.   Zucchini Muffins

Preparation Time: 10 minutes

Cooking Time: 20 minutes

Servings: 12 muffins

Ingredients:

- 2 cups zucchini, grated
- 1 cup flour, whole-wheat
- 1 cup (all-purpose) flour
- 1 tsp baking powder
- 1 tsp cinnamon, ground
- ½ tsp salt
- 1 tsp baking soda
- ¼ cup avocado/grapeseed oil
- ½ cup maple syrup
- ½ cup (unsweetened) non-dairy milk
- 2 large eggs
- 1 tsp vanilla extract, pure

Directions:

1. Turn the oven on to 375°F. A 12-cup muffin tray should be lined with silicone or paper liners.
2. To remove extra moisture, gently press the shredded zucchini between paper towels. Leave it alone.
3. Mix the all-purpose flour, whole-wheat flour, baking soda, baking powder, salt and cinnamon in a large basin.
4. Whisk the milk, eggs, vanilla, oil and maple syrup in a medium basin. With a wooden spoon, blend the egg mixture with the flour mixture. The zucchini should be gently folded in until barely combined.
5. The muffin tops should feel firm to the touch after 20 to 25 minutes of baking after equally dividing the mixture among the muffin cups.
6. Place the muffins in a large storage container when they have cooled.

Nutrition:

Nutritional Info (per serving)				
Calories	*Fat*	*Carbs*	*Fiber*	*Protein*
1876	57 g	191 g	0 g	63 g

19.   Breakfast Omelet

Preparation Time: 5 minutes

Cooking Time: 10 minutes

Servings: 2

Ingredients:

- 2 beaten eggs
- 1 stalk green onion, sliced
- ½ cup mushrooms, sliced
- 1 red bell pepper, cubed
- 1 tsp herb seasoning

Directions:

1. Place the eggs in a dish. Add the remaining ingredients into a small baking pan. Place it in the basket.
2. Cook for 10 minutes at 350°F in an oven.

Nutrition:

Nutritional Info (per serving)				
Calories	*Fat*	*Carbs*	*Sodium*	*Protein*
943	43 g	35 g	23 mg	28 g

20.   Breakfast Casserole

Preparation Time: 10 minutes

Cooking Time: 10 minutes

Servings: 4

Ingredients:

- 1 lb hash browns
- 1 lb lean breakfast sausage, crumbled
- 1 yellow onion, sliced
- 1 red bell pepper, sliced
- 1 yellow bell pepper, sliced
- 1 green bell pepper, sliced
- Pepper

Directions:

1. Cook the hash browns, Sausage and vegetables for 10 minutes at 355°F.
2. Add pepper and stir till it is completely cooked

Nutrition:

Nutritional Info (per serving)				
Calories	Fat	Carbs	Sodium	Protein
2348	36 g	157 g	21 mg	96 g

21.   Breakfast Strata

Preparation Time: 20 minutes

Cooking Time: 1 hour 15 minutes

Servings: 8

Ingredients:

- 1 lb casings removed from the sausage
- 2 cups fresh mushrooms sliced
- 10 cups day-old bread cubed
- 3 cups whole milk
- 1 ½ cup Forest ham cubed Black
- 1 package frozen thawed and drained, chopped spinach
- 2 Tbsp flour all-purpose
- 2 Tbsp powdered mustard
- 1 tsp salt
- 3 tsp melted butter
- 2 tsp basil dried

Directions:

1. Oil a 9 by 13-inch casserole dish very lightly.
2. The sausage should be cooked and stirred for about 10 minutes or until crumbled and well-browned. Place the cooked sausage in the casserole dish that has been set aside.
3. Cook and stir the mushrooms in a skillet over medium heat for 5–10 minutes, or until liquid is released and they are lightly browned; drain.
4. Except for the sausage, combine all the ingredients in a large mixing basin and toss well. After that, add the mixture on top. Place the casserole dish in the refrigerator overnight or for at least 2 hours.
5. Turn the oven temperature to 350°F (175°C).
6. Bake in a preheated oven for 60 to 70 minutes or until a knife inserted in the middle comes out clean.

Nutrition:

Nutritional Info (per serving)				
Calories	*Fat*	*Carbs*	*Fiber*	*Protein*
2980	110 g	232 g	0 g	145 g

22.   Amaranth Porridge with Pears

Preparation Time: 5 minutes

Cooking Time: 15 minutes

Servings: 2 bowls

Ingredients:

Porridge:

- ½ cup water
- ½ cup amaranth (uncooked, drained, and rinsed)
- ¼ tsp salt
- 1 cup skim milk
- 1 pear

- 1 tsp maple syrup
- ½ tsp cinnamon (ground)
- ⅛ tsp nutmeg (ground)
- ¼ tsp ginger (ground)
- ⅛ tsp clove (ground)

Topping:

- 2 Tbsp pecan pieces
- 1 cup 0% Greek yogurt (plain)
- 1 tsp maple syrup (pure)

Directions:

1. Preheat the oven to 400°F.
2. Line Parchment paper on a baking sheet. Put the porridge ingredients in a medium saucepan. Boil.
3. Cool it down. Simmer for 25 minutes. Dispose of. Layout the pecans on the baking pan.
4. Put maple syrup. Then, arrange the chopped pears next to the pecans. Maple syrup on the pears.

   15 minutes in the oven. Add pears to the cereal.

5. There is no need for topping. Divide it between the two bowls. Fill each bowl with porridge.
6. Top with pecans and the remainder of the pears. Serve.

Nutrition:

Nutritional Info (per serving)				
Calories	*Fat*	*Carbs*	*Sodium*	*Protein*
876	19 g	75 g	196 mg	29 g

23.   Sweet Potato Breakfast Bowl

Preparation Time: 5 minutes

Cooking Time: 0 minutes

Servings: 1

Ingredients:

- 1 banana (sliced)
- 1 sweet potato (pre-baked)
- ¼ cup raspberries
- 1 serving protein powder (scoop)
- ¼ cup blueberries

Toppings:

- Chia seeds
- Cacao nibs
- Favorite nuts
- Hemp hearts

Directions:

1. Mash the sweet potato in a bowl. Add the protein powder. Mix bananas, blueberries and raspberries, then the toppings. Serve.

Nutrition:

Nutritional Info (per serving)				
Calories	Fat	Carbs	Sodium	Protein
765	16 g	82 g	176 mg	11 g

Chapter #3: Appetizers and Snacks

24.   Warm Lentil salad

Preparation Time: 10 minutes

Servings: 2

Ingredients:

- 1 ¼ cup dried lentils
- 1 ¾ cup Vegetable broth, yeast-free
- ½ lemon
- 2 cloves garlic
- 1 onion
- 1 pepper or capsicum
- 4 tomatoes, skinned
- 1 courgette or zucchini
- A handful coriander or basil
- Sprinkle seeds
- Coconut oil

Directions:

1. Start by simmering the lentils with a half-squeezed lemon in a vegetable stockpot. Simmer for around 30 minutes; if required, add more stock to keep the mixture from boiling dry.
2. The onion should next be gently sautéed in coconut oil until transparent. The only things that may render coconut oil toxic are heat, light, and air. Even if you don't have coconut oil, you may steam fry using olive oil.
3. Before incorporating the peppers, courgette and garlic, the onion should first soften. Don't let everything go too mushy; everything should still be slightly crisp. Cook the tomatoes for a few minutes or until they are tender.
4. You're finished! You must season the lentils, herbs and seeds to taste.

Nutrition:

Nutritional Info (per serving)				
Calories	*Fat*	*Carbs*	*Fiber*	*Protein*
357	12 g	69 g	60 g	16 g

25.   Skewers of Vegetables and Tofu

Preparation Time: 5 minutes

Cooking Time: 5 minutes

Servings: 6

Ingredients:

- 7 oz smoked tofu
- 2 courgettes
- 1 red onion
- 1 red pepper
- 2 Tbsp olive oil
- 1 pinch salt
- 1 spicy pinch red pepper

Directions:

1. Cut the tofu into cubes and brown it for 5 minutes in a non-stick pan with a Tbsp of oil.
2. Cut the courgettes and red onions into slices, the red pepper in squares and with the help of a kitchen brush, grease them with the oil previously mixed with the salt and chili pepper..
3. Grill the courgettes without letting them burn. Place a cube of tofu alternating with a slice of courgette on a skewer toothpick and repeat.
4. Continue until all ingredients are consumed.

Nutrition:

Nutritional Info (per serving)				
Calories	*Fat*	*Carbs*	*Fiber*	*Protein*
227	6 g	5 g	0 g	10 g

26.   Baked Zucchini

Preparation Time: 10 minutes

Cooking Time: 20 minutes

Servings: 4

Ingredients:

- 4 zucchinis, quartered lengthwise
- ½ tsp thyme, dried
- ½ tsp oregano, dried
- ½ cup low-fat parmesan, grated
- ½ tsp basil, dried
- ¼ tsp garlic powder
- 2 Tbsp essential olive oil
- 2 Tbsp parsley, chopped
- A pinch black pepper

Directions:

1. Arrange zucchini pieces having a lined baking sheet; add thyme, oregano, basil, garlic powder, oil, parsley and black pepper, and toss well.
2. Sprinkle parmesan ahead, introduce within the oven, and bake at 350°F for 20 roughly minutes.
3. Divide between plates and serve as a side dish.
4. Enjoy!

Nutrition:

Nutritional Info (per serving)				
Calories	*Fat*	*Carbs*	*Fiber*	*Protein*
216	4 g	14 g	4 g	16 g

27.   Parmesan Sprinkled Garlic Beans

Preparation Time: 20 minutes

Cooking Time: 20 minutes

Servings: 4

Ingredients:

- 1 ½ lb Trimmed green beans
- 3 Tbsp olive oil
- 4 garlic cloves, minced
- 2 Tbsp grated parmesan
- ½ tsp red pepper flakes

Directions:

1. Cover the beans with water in a pot and simmer over medium-high for 5 minutes.
2. Remove the water and set aside in a bowl.
3. Pour oil in over medium-high and add pepper flakes, garlic and beans, and cook for 6 minutes.
4. Serve topped with parmesan.

Nutrition:

Nutritional Info (per serving)				
Calories	Fat	Carbs	Fiber	Protein
453	8 g	161 g	6 g	26 g

28.   Roast Green Beans with Cranberries

Preparation Time: 30 minutes

Cooking Time: 30 minutes

Servings: 4

Ingredients:

- 2 lb Halved green beans
- ¼ cup Dried cranberries
- ¼ cup Chopped almonds
- 3 Tbsp Olive oil
- Salt, to taste
- Black pepper, to taste

Directions:

1. Arrange the green beans on a baking sheet and sprinkle oil, salt and pepper on it.
2. Mix and roast in the oven for 15 minutes at 425°F.
3. Stir in the almonds and cranberries, and cook for 5 minutes.
4. Serve.

Nutrition:

Nutritional Info (per serving)				
Calories	*Fat*	*Carbs*	*Fiber*	*Protein*
376	3 g	76 g	5 g	16 g

29.   Roasted Cheesy Mushrooms

Preparation Time: 25 minutes

Cooking Time: 20 minutes

Servings: 4

Ingredients:

- 1 ½ lb Sliced cremini mushrooms
- 1 lemon zest, grated
- ¼ cup grated parmesan
- 2 tsp dried thyme
- 3 garlic cloves, Minced
- ¼ cup lemon juice
- 3 Tbsp olive oil
- Salt
- Black pepper

Directions:

1. Coat a baking dish with oil and mix mushrooms with zest, juice, Parmesan, thyme, salt, pepper and garlic.
2. Bake in the oven for 15 minutes at 375°F.
3. Serve.

Nutrition:

Nutritional Info (per serving)				
Calories	*Fat*	*Carbs*	*Fiber*	*Protein*
265	11 g	212 g	7 g	23 g

30.   Sweets with Carrots and Chocolate

Preparation Time: 20 minutes

Cooking Time: 25 minutes

Servings: 4

Ingredients:

- 4 Tbsp maple syrup
- ½ cup wholemeal flour
- ½ cup almond flour
- 3 Tbsp raw cocoa powder
- 1 tsp ground cinnamon
- The zest of an organic lemon
- 2 organic eggs
- 3 Tbsp ghee
- 4 Tbsp coconut milk
- 2 cups grated carrots
- 1 tsp baking soda
- 1 tsp cardamom
- 1 pinch salt

Directions:

1. In a bowl, mix the flours with the baking soda, cardamom, cocoa, cinnamon and lemon zest.
2. Beat the eggs with the coconut milk, carrots, salt and maple syrup.
3. Combine the 2 compounds and mix well.
4. Fill the muffin tins three-quarters full and bake in a hot oven at 350°F for about 25 minutes.

Nutrition:

Nutritional Info (per serving)				
Calories	*Fat*	*Carbs*	*Fiber*	*Protein*
773	35 g	212 g	7 g	23 g

31.   Chestnut Panini with Fennels

Preparation Time: 15 minutes

Cooking Time: 30 minutes

Servings: 5

Ingredients:

- ¾ cup boiled chestnuts
- 1 Tbsp goji berries
- 1 Tbsp olive oil
- 1 shallot
- 100 g fennel
- 2 tsp dried sage
- 2 tsp organic lemon zest
- ½ cup orange juice
- ½ cup grated quinoa bread (see recipe)
- 5 pecans with pellicle
- 1 organic egg
- 1 cup blueberries

Directions:

1. Put the goji berries in a bowl of cold water for 10 minutes and drain well after.
2. In a non-stick pan, heat the oil and brown the shallot with the chopped fennel for 5 minutes, add a few Tbsp of boiling water, and continue cooking until soft.
3. Put the boiled chestnuts in a bowl, add the soaked goji berries, the browned fennel and shallot, the orange juice, the blueberries, the lemon zest, the chopped walnuts and the beaten egg.
4. Grease a loaf pan with oil and pour the dough. Level with the back of a spoon soaked in cold water and sprinkle with grated quinoa bread. Heat the oven to 350°F and bake for about 30 minutes…. Then cut into slices!!

Nutrition:

Nutritional Info (per serving)				
Calories	*Fat*	*Carbs*	*Fiber*	*Protein*
855	26 g	182 g	0 g	56 g

32.   Coleslaw Zing

Preparation Time: 15 minutes

Cooking Time: 0 minutes

Servings: 2

Ingredients:

- ½ red cabbage
- ½ green cabbage
- 1 carrot
- 1 courgette
- ½ lime
- A handful parsley
- 1 chili, small (optional)
- 2 Tbsp olive/ Udo's Choice/avocado oil
- Himalayan salt

Directions:

1. Thinly sliced or grated vegetables such as cabbage, carrots and courgette should be used.
2. Mix the parsley, chili, lime juice, salt and oil in a bowl.
3. To serve, wait till it has cooled.

Nutrition:

Nutritional Info (per serving)				
Calories	*Fat*	*Carbs*	*Fiber*	*Protein*
538	10 g	83 g	0 g	12 g

33.   Broad Beans Salad with Turmeric Tomatoes

Preparation Time: 25 minutes

Cooking Time: 10 minutes

Servings: 2

Ingredients:

- 5 Tbsp coconut oil/olive oil
- ½ cup broad beans
- ½ sliced onion
- 1 handful cherry tomatoes
- Pinch Himalayan salt or sea
- ¾ cup new potatoes, sliced
- 1 tsp turmeric
- 1 handful each basil, parsley, and chives, all chopped

Directions:

1. Start by cooking the beans and broad onion in two Tbsp of coconut oil for around 2 minutes. If you don't have coconut oil, you can use olive oil, but I advise against it since it's the only secure cooking oil.
2. Before serving, let the beans and onion cool down a bit.
3. The tomatoes should be sliced in half, seasoned with salt and oil, and then placed on a counter to cool.
4. The young potatoes are then parboiled. Add the turmeric and bring the mixture to a boil in a pot. After 8 minutes of boiling, drain. To produce wholesome, chunky chip slices, fry them in more coconut oil for 5 minutes.
5. Before serving, drizzle some olive oil over the dish and sprinkle on some salt. Potatoes, broad beans and tomatoes are combined with herbs.

Nutrition:

Nutritional Info (per serving)				
Calories	*Fat*	*Carbs*	*Fiber*	*Protein*
348	12 g	125 g	0 g	18 g

34.   Lime Cilantro Rice

Preparation Time: 5 minutes

Cooking Time: 20 minutes

Servings: 2

Ingredients:

- ¾ cup White rice
- 1 ½ cup water
- ¼ tsp Bay leaf (ground)
- 1 Tbsp Lime juice
- 1 ½ Tbsp Olive oil
- ¼ tsp Lime Zest
- ¼ cups cilantro (chopped)

Directions:

1. In a medium-sized saucepan, combine the white rice and water, and bring to a boil over medium heat.
2. Simmer and cover the saucepan with a lid until all the water has been absorbed, around 18 to 20 minutes.
3. After the white rice has been cooked, stir in the ground bay leaf, olive oil, lime juice, lemon juice, lime zest and cilantro. This should be done using a fork rather than a spoon since this will fluff the rice rather than compress it.
4. Serve when still hot.

Nutrition:

Nutritional Info (per serving)				
Calories	Fat	Carbs	Sodiun	Protein
210	5 g	60 g	5 g	5 g

35.   Spicy Mushroom Stir Fry

Preparation Time: 10 minutes

Cooking Time: 12 minutes

Servings: 4

Ingredients:

- 1 cup low-sodium vegetable broth
- 2 Tbsp cornstarch
- 1 red bell pepper (chopped)
- 1 tsp low-sodium soy sauce
- ⅛ tsp cayenne pepper
- 2 Tbsp olive oil
- ½ tsp ground ginger
- 2 (8-oz) packages sliced button mushrooms
- 1 jalapeño pepper (minced)

Directions:

1. Combine the broth, ginger, soy sauce, cornstarch and cayenne pepper in a small bowl. After that, put it away.
2. Then, heat the olive oil in a wok (or a heavy skillet) over high heat.
3. Afterward, toss in the mushrooms and peppers. Stir-frying the veggies for 3–5 minutes, or until they are tender-crisp.
4. Stir the broth mixture into the wok and cook for an additional 3–5 minutes, or until the veggies are cooked and the sauce has thickened. Serve.

Nutrition:

Nutritional Info (per serving)				
Calories	*Fat*	*Carbs*	*Sodium*	*Protein*
456	12 g	75 g	56 g	14 g

36.   Eggs Creamy Melt Cheese

Preparation Time: 6 minutes

Cooking Time: 4 minutes

Servings: 2

Ingredients:

- 2 beaten eggs
- 1 Tbsp olive oil
- Italian seasoning as required
- 1 cup shredded tofu

Directions:

1. Combine beaten eggs and Italian spice in a small bowl.
2. Toss the tofu on top. In a pan, heat the olive oil. Add the egg mixture to the pan.
3. Cook for a total of 4 minutes.
4. Serve.

Nutrition:

Nutritional Info (per serving)				
Calories	Fat	Carbs	Sodium	Protein
421	23 g	6 g	78 g	21 g

37.   Cauliflower Mash

Preparation Time: 5 minutes

Cooking Time: 10 minutes

Servings: 4

Ingredients:

- 2 cups "leached" potatoes
- 2 Tbsp softened butter
- ¾ cup tepid low-fat milk
- 2 cups cauliflower florets
- 1 tsp ground black pepper

Directions:

1. The potatoes should be quartered. Break apart the cauliflower.
2. In a large saucepan of boiling water, add the vegetables. Cook for approximately 10 minutes, or until the vegetables are soft.
3. Drain after removing the pan from the heat. Add the milk, butter and pepper to taste.
4. Cream the vegetables using an immersion blender.
5. Serve immediately.

Nutrition:

Nutritional Info (per serving)				
Calories	Fat	Carbs	Sodium	Protein
365	15 g	67 g	49 mg	19 g

38.   Jalapeno Crisp

Preparation Time: 10 minutes

Cooking Time: 1 hour 15 minutes

Servings: 20

Ingredients:

- ½ cup sesame seeds
- ½ cup hulled hemp seeds
- 3 Tbsp Psyllium husk
- ½ cup flax seeds
- 1 tsp salt
- 1 tsp baking powder
- ½ cup sunflower seeds
- 2 cups water

Directions:

1. Preheat the oven to 350°F.
2. Combine seeds, baking powder, salt and Psyllium husk in a blender. Blend until you have a sand-like texture, then add the water and blend till you get a batter.
3. Allow the batter to rest for 10 minutes or until it forms a thick dough-like substance.
4. Whip the dough and place it on a parchment-lined cookie sheet. Spread it out evenly, ensuring a thickness of ¼ inch all the way around. In your oven, bake for 75 minutes.
5. Remove the spices and chop them into 20 pieces. Allow 30 minutes for cooling before serving.

Nutrition:

Nutritional Info (per serving)				
Calories	*Fat*	*Carbs*	*Sodium*	*Protein*
654	**61 g**	**59 g**	**60 mg**	**47 g**

39.   Apple Brie Pizza

Preparation Time: 10 minutes

Cooking Time: 15 minutes

Servings: 12

Ingredients:

Pizza crust:

- ½ cup hot water
- 1 ¼ cup all-purpose flour
- 1 tsp instant yeast
- 4 tsp canola oil
- 2 tsp cornmeal

Toppings:

- 7 oz Brie cheese with rind (softened)
- 1 tsp apple juice
- 2 Tbsp light sour cream
- ¼ tsp dill weed
- 1–2 red apples (with peel, cut into paper-thin wedges)
- 2 tsp Parmesan cheese (grated)

Directions:

1. Fill a food processor halfway with flour and yeast. Pour hot water and frying oil into the food chute with the cover on and the machine running. For approximately 50 seconds, process until the ball forms. Remove the dough from the pan and cover it in plastic wrap. Allow for a 10-minute rest period. Alternatively, you may mix the dough by hand if you don't have a food processor. Preheat the oven to 450°F.
2. Separate the dough into two equal parts. Sprinkle 1 tsp cornmeal on the work surface, 1 part of the dough should be rolled out to a 10" diameter on cornmeal. Rep with the remaining dough part. Place on a baking sheet that has been buttered. With a fork, poke holes all over the dough. Bake each crust for approximately 10 minutes on the bottom rack. These may be baked one at a time. Before adding toppings to the pizza crusts, allow them to cool.

Toppings:

1. On a large platter, mash Brie cheese, sour cream, dill weed and apple juice with a fork. Rather than mashing until smooth, mix roughly. Apply to both crusts.
2. Place a single layer of apple slices on top of each crust. Parmesan cheese should be sprinkled on top. Bake for approximately 5 minutes in the center of a 450°F oven or until the crust is crisp and the top is starting to become golden. To make a total of 24 wedges, cut each pizza into 12 wedges.

Nutrition:

Nutritional Info (per serving)				
Calories	Fat	Carbs	Sodium	Protein
2235	26 g	320 g	135 mg	85 g

40.   Roasted Broccoli

Preparation Time: 5 minutes

Cooking Time: 15 minutes

Servings: 6

Ingredients:

- 4 tsp honey
- 3 Tbsp olive oil, extra-virgin
- 8 cups broccoli florets
- 1 Tbsp lemon juice
- 1 tsp powdered garlic
- ¼ tsp salt
- 2 tsp chipotles in adobo, cannoned and minced

Directions:

1. Set the oven temperature to 425°F. Coat a large baking sheet with a rim with cooking spray.
2. Combine the honey, oil, lemon juice, chipotles, garlic powder and salt in a sizable mixing bowl. Add the broccoli and toss to coat.
3. When browned and soft in spots, add to the prepared baking sheet and cook for 12–15 minutes, stirring once.

Nutrition:

Nutritional Info (per serving)				
Calories	*Fat*	*Carbs*	*Fiber*	*Protein*
221	**7 g**	**63 g**	**0 g**	**47 g**

41.   Buffalo-chicken Dip

Preparation Time: 5 minutes

Cooking Time: 7 minutes

Servings: 10

Ingredients:

- 8 oz coconut cream, non-dairy
- 2 cups chicken, cooked and shredded.
- 1 cup (vegan) blue cheese, non-dairy
- ½ cup buffalo-hot sauce

Directions:

1. In a 7" glass bowl, mix the spicy sauce, coconut cream, chicken and blue cheese dressing. Stir everything together completely.
2. Put 1 cup of water in the inner pot and place the steam rack inside. On top of the bowl, place the steam rack. Put the lid on.
3. By tapping the Manual or Pressure Cook button, you can set the time to 7 minutes.
4. When the timer goes off, let the pressure go down naturally till the float valve drops before opening the lid.
5. Stir the dip before serving it warm.

Nutrition:

Nutritional Info (per serving)				
Calories	*Fat*	*Carbs*	*Fiber*	*Protein*
437	17 g	8 g	0 g	48 g

42.   Mexican Layer Dip

Preparation Time: 10 minutes

Cooking Time: 0 minutes

Servings: 15

Ingredients:

- 1 Tbsp lemon juice
- A 15-oz can beans
- ½ cup cream
- 3 avocados
- ½ cup plum tomato
- ½ cup cheese
- 1 Tbsp mayonnaise
- 2 Tbsp fresh cilantro
- 3 Tbsp taco seasoning
- Mashed potatoes 2 pounds
- ½ cup diced onion
- 2 bell peppers
- 2 to 3 cups lettuce

Directions:

1. Evenly put the ingredients in a baking pan.
2. The refried black beans are the first layer. 2nd layer: mayonnaise, lemon juice, and mashed potatoes with ripe avocados. Layer 3: Combine sour cream, cilantro and reduced-sodium taco seasoning. Peppers (bell) (layer 4) (layer 5) shredded cheese, shredded lettuce (layer 6), 7th layer: diced plum tomato and onion.

Nutrition:

Nutritional Info (per serving)				
Calories	*Fat*	*Carbs*	*Fiber*	*Protein*
996	37 g	163 g	0 g	43 g

43.   Grilled Sweet Potatoes and Scallions

Preparation Time: 10 minutes

Cooking Time: 15 minutes

Servings: 4

Ingredients:

- 4 potatoes
- 2 Tbsp Dijon mustard
- 8 medium scallions
- 2 tsp honey
- ¾ cup olive oil
- ¼ cup balsamic vinegar
- Freshly ground pepper, to taste
- ¼ cup parsley

Directions:

1. Preheat the grill to medium-high. Brush the potatoes and onions with oil before placing them on the grill.
2. Place them on the grill for 3 to 4 minutes on each side, or until the potatoes are just tender. The scallions should be grilled until tender and marked.
3. Remove the scallions from the grill and slice them thinly. Combine ½ cup olive oil, mustard, ¼ cup of vinegar and the honey in a large mixing basin. Season with pepper to taste. Toss in the potatoes, scallions and parsley until well coated.
4. Serve immediately on a plate.

Nutrition:

Nutritional Info (per serving)				
Calories	Fat	Carbs	Sodium	Protein
570	41 g	96 g	257 mg	15 g

44.   Garlicky Dill Cucumber and Yogurt Dip

Preparation Time: 15 minutes

Cooking Time: 1 minute

Servings: 4

Ingredients:

- 2 Tbsp extra-virgin olive oil
- 1 cucumber, peeled and shredded
- 1 cup plain coconut yogurt
- 1 garlic clove, minced
- 1 scallion, chopped
- 2 Tbsp chopped fresh dill
- 1 tsp salt
- 2 Tbsp freshly squeezed lemon juice

Directions:

1. In a fine-mesh strainer, add the shredded cucumber and drain it.
2. Add the yogurt, garlic, scallion, dill, salt and lemon juice into a small bowl, and stir them together.
3. Stir in the drained cucumber, then transfer them into a serving bowl.
4. Drizzle with the olive oil before serving.

Nutrition:

Nutritional Info (per serving)				
Calories	*Fat*	*Carbs*	*Fiber*	*Protein*
876	19 g	47 g	0 g	5 g

45.   Healthy Trail Mix

Preparation Time: 5 minutes

Cooking Time: 0

Servings: 6

Ingredients:

- 1 cup sunflower seeds
- 1 cup pumpkin seeds
- 1 cup dried cranberries
- 1 cup raisins
- 1 cup large coconut flakes
- ½ cup cacao nibs (optional)

Directions:

1. Add the sunflower seeds, pumpkin seeds, cranberries, raisins, coconut and cacao nibs (if using) to a large bowl, and stir them together.
2. Place the mixture into large jars, and store covered in a cool, dry place. Or portion into small containers for a quick grab-and-go option.

Nutrition:

Nutritional Info (per serving)				
Calories	*Fat*	*Carbs*	*Fiber*	*Protein*
1183	81 g	69 g	0 g	35 g

Chapter #4: Soups, Salads and Sides

46.   Farro Salad with Arugula

Preparation Time: 10 minutes

Cooking Time: 35 minutes

Servings: 2

Ingredients:

- ½ cup farro
- 1 ½ cup chicken stock
- 1 tsp salt
- ½ tsp ground black pepper
- 2 cups arugula, chopped
- 1 cucumber, chopped
- 1 Tbsp lemon juice
- ½ tsp olive oil
- ½ tsp Italian seasoning

Directions:

1. Combine farro, salt and chicken stock and transfer the mixture to a pan. Secure the lid and boil it for 35 minutes.
2. Meanwhile, set all the remaining ingredients in the salad bowl. Chill the farro and add it to the salad bowl too.
3. Mix the salad well.

Nutrition:

Nutritional Info (per serving)				
Calories	*Fat*	*Carbs*	*Fiber*	*Protein*
296	2 g	148 g	12 g	5 g

47. Easy Tomato Chickpea Salad

Preparation Time: 10 minutes

Cooking Time: 6 minutes

Servings: 4

Ingredients:

- 2 Tbsp olive oil
- 15 oz canned chickpeas, drained and rinsed
- 2 pints cherry tomatoes, halved
- 2 tsp ground cumin
- ¼ cup chopped parsley
- A pinch salt and black pepper

For the Vinaigrette:

- 2 Tbsp olive oil
- 1 tsp minced shallot
- 1 Tbsp sherry vinegar

Directions:

1. Heat a pan with 2 Tbsp oil over medium-high heat and add the chickpeas.
2. Spread the chickpeas evenly in the pan and cook for 4 minutes. Add the cumin, salt and pepper, and toss a bit then cook for 2 minutes more.
3. Remove from heat and cool down, then transfer to a bowl. Add the tomatoes and the parsley, and toss. In another bowl, whisk together the 2 Tbsp of oil with shallot and vinegar, and pour over the salad.
4. Toss well and serve as a side dish.
5. Enjoy!

Nutrition:

Nutritional Info (per serving)				
Calories	*Fat*	*Carbs*	*Fiber*	*Protein*
573	**16 g**	**168 g**	**23 g**	**35 g**

48.   Chicken and Pea Soup

Preparation Time: 20 minutes

Cooking Time: 30 minutes

Servings: 4

Ingredients:

- 1 Tbsp olive oil
- 1 peeled and coarsely chopped small onion
- 1/3 lb cooked leftover chicken, coarsely chopped
- 2 cups fresh chicken stock
- 1 cup peas, frozen
- Ground black pepper, to taste.

Directions:

1. Take a nonstick saucepan, heat the oil, and then add the onion and cook, often turning, for 3–4 minutes or until softened.
2. Sprinkle with ground black pepper and bring the chicken, stock and peas to a boil. Cook, stirring periodically, for 5 minutes.
3. Serve immediately in two hot bowls.

Nutrition:

Nutritional Info (per serving)				
Calories	Fat	Carbs	Sodium	Protein
769	12 g	90 g	143 g	46 g

49.   Chicken and Lentil Soup

Preparation Time: 20 minutes

Cooking Time: 30 minutes

Servings: 4

Ingredients:

- 1 Tbsp coconut or olive oil
- 1 medium peeled and coarsely chopped onion
- 1 pepper, seeded and cut into 1/2-inch cubes, any color
- 2 Tbsp curry powder (medium)
- 14 oz can tomatoes, chopped
- 4 cups chicken stock
- 50 g red split lentils, dry
- 4 cups water
- Ground black pepper, to taste
- Pinch salt
- 1 cup spinach, frozen
- ½ lb cooked chicken, cut roughly
- Serve with lemon wedges.

Directions:

1. Take a large nonstick saucepan, heat the oil, add the onion and pepper, and cook for 5 minutes until it becomes softened.
2. Cook for a few more seconds after adding the curry powder. Bring to a boil with the tomatoes.
3. Stir for a few minutes more, then add the chicken broth.
4. Wash the lentils with fresh water and place them in the pan with the frozen spinach. Bring to low heat.
5. Season with a generous amount of crushed black pepper and a pinch of sea salt. Cook, occasionally stirring, for 10 minutes.

6. Cook and occasionally stir for at least 8 to 10 minutes, or until the lentils are mushy and the spinach has thawed. If the soup becomes too sticky, add a little bit more water.

7. Season to taste, then serve deep dishes with lemon wedges to squeeze over the top.

Nutrition:

Nutritional Info (per serving)				
Calories	Fat	Carbs	Sodium	Protein
1955	16 g	127 g	48 g	86 g

50.   Tomato Soup

Preparation Time: 10 minutes

Cooking Time: 20 minutes

Servings: 2

Ingredients:

- 14 oz can tomatoes, chopped
- ½ can cannellini beans, drained
- 2 clipped and coarsely chopped spring onions
- ¼ cup creamy light cheese
- Salt and ground black pepper, to taste
- 6 large basil leaves, with more to serve (if desired)
- 1 Tbsp olive oil
- 1 Tbsp tomato puree

Directions:

1. In a blender, combine all the ingredients, sprinkle with sea salt and plenty of ground black pepper, and mix until smooth.
2. Transfer to a nonstick saucepan, add enough water to get your desired consistency, and gently cook through.
3. Salt to taste and serve in bowls or cups, garnished with basil leaves if desired.

Nutrition:

Nutritional Info (per serving)				
Calories	*Fat*	*Carbs*	*Sodium*	*Protein*
997	10 g	121 g	78 mg	48 g

51. Spicy Pepper Soup

Preparation Time: 10 minutes

Cooking Time: 45 minutes

Servings: 4

Ingredients:

- 8 crumbled red peppers
- 1 red onion, trimmed in half
- 2 crumbled garlic cloves
- 3 cups chicken broth.
- 2 habanero chili with stems removed and crumbled
- 2 ½ Tbsp olive oil

Directions:

1. Cook the olive oil in a skillet at low heat, then include the onions and peppers, simmering for around 5 minutes. Sauté for 3–4 minutes with the garlic cloves and chilies.
2. Allow the broth to boil before lowering the heat and simmering for 30 minutes. Let it cool. In a food grinder, grind the ingredients until smooth.
3. Serve with black pepper and lime zest.

Nutrition:

Nutritional Info (per serving)				
Calories	*Fat*	*Carbs*	*Sodium*	*Protein*
372	8 g	136 g	98 mg	9 g

52.   Chicken Noodle Soup

Preparation Time: 15 minutes

Cooking Time: 45 minutes

Servings: 8

Ingredients:

- 1 lb chicken parts
- 1 tsp red pepper
- ¼ cup lemon juice
- 1 tsp caraway seed
- 3 ½ cups water
- 1 tsp oregano
- 1 Tbsp poultry seasoning
- 1 tsp sugar
- 1 tsp garlic powder
- ½ cup celery
- 1 tsp onion powder
- ½ cup green pepper
- 2 Tbsp vegetable oil
- 1 cup egg noodles
- 1 tsp black pepper

Directions:

1. The lemon juice should be applied to the chicken pieces.
2. Combine vegetable oil, black pepper, red pepper, caraway seed, oregano and sugar in a large saucepan.
3. Cook until the chicken is cooked through.
4. Cook for another 15 minutes, after adding the other ingredients, and serve immediately.

Nutrition:

Nutritional Info (per serving)				
Calories	*Fat*	*Carbs*	*Fiber*	*Protein*
996	37 g	163 g	0 g	43 g

53.   Salad with Strawberries and Feta Cheese

Preparation Time: 20 minutes

Cooking Time: 0 minutes

Servings: 2

Ingredients:

- Baby lettuce (to taste)
- 1 pint strawberries
- 2 Tbsp extra-virgin olive oil
- ¼ tsp black pepper
- 2-oz feta cheese
- Balsamic vinegar as required

Directions:

1. The lettuce should be washed and dried before cutting the strawberries.
2. Cut the feta cheese into 8 pieces. Whisk the balsamic vinegar and extra-virgin olive oil in a large mixing bowl.
3. Combine the strawberries in a bowl, crush them, and add the dressing; divide the lettuce among four plates and chop the remaining strawberries, laying them over the salad. Add cheese slices and pepper on top.
4. Serve and have fun.

Nutrition:

Calories	Fat	Carbs	Sodium	Protein
Nutritional Info (per serving)				
1110	27 g	86 g	42 mg	15 g

54.   Tropical Chicken Salad

Preparation Time: 5 minutes

Cooking Time: 20 minutes

Servings: 6

Ingredients:

- 1 lb boneless, skinless chicken breast
- 2 Tbsp apple cider vinegar
- Juice 1 freshly squeezed lime
- 2 Tbsp olive oil
- ¼ cup chopped fresh cilantro
- ½ tsp ground white pepper
- 1 ripe mango, diced
- 1 small red onion, diced
- 1 small bell pepper, diced
- 1 jalapeño pepper, minced
- 2 cloves garlic, minced
- 1 cup cooked no-salt-added black beans

Directions:

1. Place the chicken breast into a pot and add enough water to cover.
2. Bring to a boil over high heat. Once boiling, reduce the heat slightly, and continue boiling for about 20 minutes until fully cooked.
3. Remove from the heat, drain, and set aside to cool. While the chicken is cooling, place the vinegar, lime juice, olive oil, cilantro and white pepper into a small bowl and whisk well to combine.
4. Once the chicken is cool to touch, cut it into bite-sized pieces. Place into a mixing bowl and add the mango, onion, peppers, garlic and beans. Pour the dressing over the chicken salad and stir well to coat.
5. Serve immediately or cover and refrigerate until serving.

Nutrition:

Nutritional Info (per serving)				
Calories	*Fat*	*Carbs*	*Sodium*	*Protein*
1238	16 g	75 g	368 mg	91 g

55.   Mayo-less Tuna Salad

Preparation Time: 10 minutes

Cooking Time: 0 minutes

Servings: 2

Ingredients:

- 5 oz tuna, canned in water, drained
- 1 cup cooked pasta
- 1 Tbsp extra-virgin olive oil
- 1 Tbsp red wine vinegar
- ¼ cup green onion, sliced
- 2 cups arugula
- 1 Tbsp parmesan cheese, shredded
- ½ tsp black pepper

Directions:

1. Toss the tuna with vinegar, arugula, oil, onion, and cooked pasta in a large bowl.
2. Divide the dish between 2 plates equally.
3. Top with pepper and parmesan before serving.
4. Serve hot.

Nutrition:

Nutritional Info (per serving)				
Calories	*Fat*	*Carbs*	*Sodium*	*Protein*
1265	12 g	119 g	824 mg	57 g

56.   Crunchy Couscous Salad

Preparation Time: 15 minutes + 1 Hour to Cool

Cooking Time: 20 minutes

Servings: 6

Ingredients:

- 6 oz fresh boneless chicken breast.
- 1 cup couscous
- 6 cups water or chicken broth with moderate salt or no salt applied
- 1 medium cucumber, scraped with contrasting green stripes, cut into quarters, and divided into slices
- 1 medium chop red bell pepper
- ¼ cup chopped parsley
- ¼ cup apple cider vinegar
- 3 Tbsp olive oil
- 1 tsp basil (preserved)
- ½ tsp black pepper
- 3 Tbsp feta cheese, crumbled

Directions:

1. Observe the package directions for cooking the couscous.
2. Meanwhile, bring the chicken breast and water to a boil in a large saucepan over high heat. Slow the heat down to a low simmer and cover the saucepan.
3. Cook for 15 minutes or until the chicken breasts are cooked through. Remove the chicken from the stove and set it aside to cool before dicing.
4. Meld the couscous, chicken breast, cucumber, bell pepper, onion and parsley in a large mixing basin.
5. Add all the ingredients, including vinegar, oil, basil and black pepper, to a new bowl and whisk them together. In a small mixing bowl, gently fold in the feta cheese.
6. Toss the couscous with the dressing until well incorporated.
7. Serve warm or cooled after 1 hour in the refrigerator. Retain leftovers refrigerated for up to 5 days in an airtight container.

Nutrition:

Nutritional Info (per serving)				
Calories	*Fat*	*Carbs*	*Sodium*	*Protein*
1655	9 g	196 g	128 mg	136 g

57. Rice and Chicken Soup

Preparation Time: 10 minutes

Cooking Time: 30 minutes

Servings: 3

Ingredients:

- 1 cup onions, chopped
- 1 cup celery, sliced
- ¾ cup uncooked white rice
- 1 cup chopped carrots
- ½ tsp pepper
- ½ tsp thyme leaves, completely dry
- 1 bay leaf
- 10 cup chicken broth (low salt)
- 2 chicken breasts, boneless and skinless, minced into cubes
- ¼ cup parsley, trimmed
- 2 Tbsp lime juice

Directions:

1. Add onion, celery, carrots, rice, chili, thyme, bay leaf and chicken stock in a large saucepan.
2. Heat to a simmer, and stir the mixture once or twice throughout the process.
3. Turn the heat low, cover, and stew for 20 minutes. Cook, uncovered, for 5–10 minutes with the chicken chunks.
4. Remove the bay leaf. Just before serving, add the parsley and lime juice.

Nutrition:

Nutritional Info (per serving)				
Calories	*Fat*	*Carbs*	*Sodium*	*Protein*
1547	37 g	146 g	52 g	57 g

58.   Garlicky Ginger Potato and Rice Soup

Preparation Time: 15 minutes

Cooking Time: 15 minutes

Servings: 4-6

Ingredients:

- 1 large sweet potato, peeled and cut into 1-inch cubes
- 4 cups vegetable broth
- 1 bunch broccolini, cut into 1-inch pieces
- 2 onions, coarsely chopped
- 2 garlic cloves, sliced thin
- 2 tsp minced fresh ginger
- 1 cup cooked Arborio rice
- ¼ cup fresh cilantro leaves

Directions:

1. Add the broth into a large Dutch oven, bringing to a boil over high heat.
2. Place the sweet potato, onion, garlic and ginger into the oven and simmer for 5 to 8 minutes, or until the sweet potato is cooked through.
3. Stir in the broccolini and simmer for another 3 minutes.
4. Take the pan off the heat. Mix in the rice and cilantro.

Nutrition:

Nutritional Info (per serving)				
Calories	*Fat*	*Carbs*	*Fiber*	*Protein*
867	6 g	289 g	0 g	18 g

59.   Collard Greens Mix

Preparation Time: 10 minutes

Cooking Time: 10 minutes

Servings: 4

Ingredients:

- 5 bunches collard greens, chopped
- Salt and black pepper, to taste
- 1 Tbsp crushed red pepper flakes
- 3 Tbsp chicken stock
- 2 Tbsp minced garlic
- ¼ cup olive oil

Directions:

1. Heat a pot with the oil over medium heat and add the garlic. Stir and cook for 2 minutes.
2. Add the collard greens, pepper flakes, stock, salt and pepper.
3. Mix well and cook for 8 minutes, then divide between plates and serve as a side dish.
4. Enjoy!

Nutrition:

Nutritional Info (per serving)				
Calories	*Fat*	*Carbs*	*Fiber*	*Protein*
356	12 g	79 g	10 g	9 g

60.   Watercress Side Salad

Preparation Time: 10 minutes

Cooking Time: 0 minutes

Servings: 4

Ingredients:

- 4 medium endives, trimmed and thinly sliced
- 1 Tbsp lemon juice
- 1 shallot, finely chopped
- 1 Tbsp balsamic vinegar
- 2 Tbsp olive oil
- 6 Tbsp coconut cream
- Salt and black pepper, to taste
- 4 oz watercress, cut into medium springs
- 1 Tbsp chopped chervil
- 1 Tbsp chopped tarragon
- 1 Tbsp chopped chives
- 1/3 cup chopped almonds
- 1 Tbsp chopped parsley

Directions:

1. In a small bowl, whisk together the lemon juice with vinegar, salt, pepper, oil and shallot, then set aside for 10 minutes.
2. In a separate salad bowl, mix the endives with watercress, chives, tarragon, parsley, chervil, cream and the lemon juice mix.
3. Toss and serve as a side dish with almonds sprinkled on top.
4. Enjoy!

Nutrition:

Nutritional Info (per serving)				
Calories	*Fat*	*Carbs*	*Fiber*	*Protein*
346	6 g	187 g	56 g	12 g

61.   Chili Eggplant Mix

Preparation Time: 10 minutes

Cooking Time: 15 minutes

Servings: 4

Ingredients:

- 1 large Asian eggplant, cubed
- 1 yellow onion, thinly sliced
- 2 Tbsp olive oil
- 2 tsp minced garlic
- 2 tsp chili paste
- ¼ cup coconut cream
- 4 green onions, chopped

Directions:

1. Heat a pan with the oil over medium-high heat, then add the onion, stir, and cook for 3–4 minutes.
2. Add the garlic, chili paste, green onions and coconut cream and stir, cooking for 2–3 minutes more.
3. Add the eggplant, toss, and cook for 7–8 minutes more.
4. Divide between plates and serve as a side dish.
5. Enjoy!

Nutrition:

Nutritional Info (per serving)				
Calories	Fat	Carbs	Fiber	Protein
162	5 g	121 g	45 g	3 g

Chapter #5: Main Dishes: Meat

62.   Pork and Creamy Veggie Sauce

Preparation Time: 10 minutes

Cooking Time: 1 hour and 20 minutes

Servings: 4

Ingredients:

- 2 lb pork roast
- 1 cup low-sodium veggie stock
- 2 carrots, chopped.
- 1 leek, chopped.
- 1 celery stalk, chopped.
- 1 tsp black peppercorns
- 2 yellow onions, cut into quarters.
- 1 Tbsp chives, chopped.
- 1 Tbsp parsley, chopped.
- 2 cups nonfat yogurt
- 1 cup coconut cream
- 1 tsp mustard
- Black pepper towards the taste

Directions:

1. Put the roast in a baking dish, add carrots, leek, celery, peppercorns, onions, stock and black pepper, cover, introduce inside oven and bake at 400°F for 60 minutes and 10 minutes.
2. Transfer the roast using a platter and all sorts of the veggies mix with a pan.
3. Heat this mixture over medium heat, add yogurt, cream and mustard, and toss cooking for 10 minutes, drizzle inside the roast, and serve.

Nutrition:

Nutritional Info (per serving)				
Calories	*Fat*	*Carbs*	*Fiber*	*Protein*
2432	48 g	132 g	21 g	92 g

63.   Ground Pork Pan

Preparation Time: 10 minutes

Cooking Time: 20 minutes

Servings: 4

Ingredients:

- 1 lemon, zest
- Juice a single lemon
- 2 garlic cloves, minced
- 1 Tbsp organic olive oil
- 1 lb pork meat, ground
- Black pepper, to taste
- 1 pint cherry tomatoes, chopped
- 1 small red onion, chopped
- ½ cup low-sodium veggie stock,
- 2 Tbsp low-sodium tomato paste
- 1 Tbsp basil, chopped

Directions:

1. Heat a pan with all the oil over medium heat, add garlic and onion, stir, and cook for 5 minutes.
2. Add pork, black pepper, tomatoes, stock, freshly squeezed lemon juice, lemon zest and tomato paste, toss, and cook for a quarter-hour.
3. Add basil, toss, divide between plates, and serve.
4. Enjoy!

Nutrition:

Nutritional Info (per serving)				
Calories	*Fat*	*Carbs*	*Fiber*	*Protein*
1987	76 g	134 g	27 g	97 g

64.   Tarragon Pork Steak

Preparation Time: 10 minutes

Cooking Time: 22 minutes

Servings: 4

Ingredients:

- 4 medium pork steaks
- Black pepper, to taste
- 1 Tbsp extra-virgin olive oil
- 8 cherry tomatoes, halved
- A handful tarragon, chopped

Directions:

1. Heat up a pan while using the oil over medium-high heat, add the steaks, and season with black pepper, cooking them for 6 minutes on each side and divide them between plates.
2. Heat the same pan over medium heat, add the tomatoes along with the tarragon, cook for 10 minutes, divide next around the pork, and serve.
3. Enjoy!

Nutrition:

Nutritional Info (per serving)				
Calories	*Fat*	*Carbs*	*Fiber*	*Protein*
765	34 g	52 g	16 g	56 g

65. Beef and Vegetable Soup

Preparation Time: 15 minutes

Cooking Time: 45 minutes

Servings: 8

Ingredients:

- 1 lb stew beef
- 3 cups water
- 1 cup onions
- ½ cup peas
- 1 tsp black pepper
- ½ cup okra
- ½ tsp basil
- ½ cup carrot
- ½ tsp thyme
- ½ cup corn

Directions:

1. Place stew, onions, the other ingredients and water in a large saucepan.
2. The cooking time is around 45 minutes. Add all the frozen veggies and cook on low heat until the meat is cooked.
3. Serve immediately.

Nutrition:

Nutritional Info (per serving)				
Calories	*Fat*	*Carbs*	*Sodium*	*Protein*
983	**30 g**	**65 g**	**102 mg**	**67 g**

66.   Chuck Roast and Veggies

Preparation Time: ten minutes

Cooking Time: 1 hour and a half-hour

Servings: 6

Ingredients:

- 3 lb lean chuck roast, fat removed
- 2 yellow onions, roughly chopped
- 1 cup low-sodium beef stock
- 1 Tbsp thyme, chopped
- 2 celery sticks, chopped
- 2 carrots, sliced
- 3 garlic cloves, minced
- A pinch black pepper

Directions:

1. In a roasting pan, combine the roast with all the onions, stock, thyme, celery, carrots, garlic, and a pinch of pepper, introduce in the oven, and roast at 400°F for 60 minutes and around 30 minutes.
2. Slice the roast, divide it, plus the veggies from a pot between plates, and serve for lunch.
3. Enjoy!

Nutrition:

Nutritional Info (per serving)				
Calories	*Fat*	*Carbs*	*Fiber*	*Protein*
2542	121 g	88 g	11 g	131 g

67.   Pork Meatballs

Preparation Time: ten minutes

Cooking Time: 10 minutes

Servings: 3

Ingredients:

- 1 lb pork, ground
- 1/3 cup cilantro, chopped
- 1 cup red onion, chopped
- 4 garlic cloves, minced
- 1 Tbsp ginger, grated
- 1 Thai chili, chopped
- 2 Tbsp extra-virgin olive oil

Directions:

1. In a bowl, combine the meat with cilantro, onion, garlic, ginger and chili, stir well, and shape medium meatballs out of this mix.
2. Heat a pan while using oil over medium-high heat, add the meatballs, and cook them for 5 minutes on either side, divide them between plates, and serve with a side salad.
3. Enjoy!

Nutrition:

Nutritional Info (per serving)				
Calories	*Fat*	*Carbs*	*Fiber*	*Protein*
765	34 g	54`` g	2 g	84 g

68.   Nutmeg Meatballs Curry

Preparation Time: 40 minutes

Cooking Time: 25 minutes

Servings: 3

Ingredients:

- 1 lb pork meat, ground
- 1 egg
- 1 Tbsp Parsley, chopped
- 2 Tbsp Coconut flour
- 1 garlic clove, minced
- Salt and black pepper, to taste
- ¼ cup veggie stock
- ½ cup tomato passata
- ¼ tsp nutmeg, ground
- ¼ tsp sweet paprika
- 1 Tbsp olive oil
- 1 carrot, chopped

Directions:

1. Thoroughly mix the meat with egg, parsley, salt, pepper, garlic, nutmeg and paprika in a suitable bowl.
2. Mix well and make small meatballs out of this mixture.
3. Cover these balls with dry flour or dust the balls with flour.
4. Place a pot with oil over medium-high heat.
5. Add the dusted meatballs to the pot and sear them for 4 minutes per side.
6. Toss in tomato passata, carrots, and stock.
7. Cover this mixture and let it simmer for 20 minutes.
8. Serve right away and devour.

Nutrition:

Nutritional Info (per serving)				
Calories	*Fat*	*Carbs*	*Fiber*	*Protein*
1256	68 g	20 g	6 g	125 g

69.   Pan-Seared Sausage and Kale

Preparation Time: 35 minutes

Cooking Time: 30 minutes

Servings: 4

Ingredients:

- 3 lb chopped kale
- 1 ½ lb Italian pork sausage: sliced
- 1 tsp minced garlic
- 1 cup water
- 1 cup chopped onion
- ½ cup red bell pepper: seeded and chopped
- ½ cup red chili pepper: chopped
- Black pepper
- Salt

Directions:

1. Put a pan on medium heat and add the sausage to brown for 10 minutes.
2. Mix in onions and cook for 3–4 minutes.
3. Add in the garlic and bell pepper, and cook for 1 minute.
4. Mix in the chili, kale, water, pepper and salt, and let cook for 10 minutes.
5. Serve

Nutrition:

Nutritional Info (per serving)				
Calories	*Fat*	*Carbs*	*Fiber*	*Protein*
1346	43 g	61 g	3 g	54 g

70.   Pork Rolls

Preparation Time: 30 minutes

Cooking Time: 30 minutes

Servings: 6

Ingredients:

- 3 peeled and minced garlic cloves
- ½ tsp Italian seasoning
- 6 prosciutto slices
- 2 Tbsp chopped fresh parsley
- 1 lb thinly sliced pork cutlets
- 1 Tbsp coconut oil
- ¼ cup chopped onion
- 15 oz canned diced tomatoes
- ⅓ cup chicken stock
- 2 Tbsp grated parmesan cheese
- ⅓ cup ricotta cheese
- Seasoning: Salt and ground black pepper

Directions:

1. Flatten pork pieces with a meat pounder.
2. Put prosciutto slices on top of each piece and then divide ricotta cheese, parsley and Parmesan cheese.
3. Each piece of pork should be rolled and secured with a toothpick.
4. With medium-high temperature, heat the oil in a pan, add pork rolls, and cook until brown on both sides, and transfer to a plate.
5. Heat the pan again over medium temperature, put onion and garlic, and mix well. Cook for 5 minutes.
6. The stock should be added and cooked for another 3 minutes.
7. Remove the toothpicks from the pork rolls and return them to the pan.
8. Put tomatoes, Italian seasoning, salt and pepper, stir, bring to a boil, reduce the heat to medium-low, cover the pan with a lid, and cook for 30 minutes.
9. Divide between plates and serve it.

Nutrition:

Nutritional Info (per serving)				
Calories	*Fat*	*Carbs*	*Fiber*	*Protein*
923	19 g	27 g	1 g	32 g

71.   Beef Stew

Preparation Time: 10 minutes

Cooking Time: 10 hours

Servings: 6

Ingredients:

- 1 ½ lb beef chuck pot roast, cubed
- 1 lb butternut squash, cubed
- 2 yellow onions, chopped
- 2 garlic cloves, minced
- 14 oz low-sodium beef stock
- 8 oz tomato sauce
- 1 tsp dry mustard
- A pinch black pepper
- A pinch allspice, ground
- 9 oz green beans

Directions:

1. In your slow cooker, combine the beef with squash, onions, garlic, stock, tomato sauce, mustard, black pepper, green beans and allspice, toss, cover, and cook on Low for 10 hours.
2. Divide into bowls and serve for lunch.
3. Enjoy!

Nutrition:

Nutritional Info (per serving)				
Calories	*Fat*	*Carbs*	*Fiber*	*Protein*
1654	54 g	58 g	8 g	148 g

72.   Lamb Chops with Redcurrant and Mint Sauce

Preparation Time: 10 minutes

Cooking Time: 40 minutes

Servings: 4

Ingredients:

- 4 Lean lamb chops
- 4 Tbsp Redcurrant jelly
- 1 Tbsp Lemon juice
- 4 Tbsp Water
- 1 Tbsp Mint sauce

Directions:

1. Combine the redcurrant jelly, mint sauce, lemon juice and water in an ovenproof dish.
2. Trim the chops and set them on the sauce-coated plate, rotating to coat each chop well.
3. Bake uncovered for 35–40 minutes at 350°F (Gas Mark 4) in a preheated oven until the lamb is cooked. Before serving, the sauce may need to be thinned with cornflour and a little water.

Nutrition:

Nutritional Info (per serving)				
Calories	*Fat*	*Carbs*	*Sodium*	*Protein*
482	15 g	25 g	166 mg	48 g

73.   Spicy Paprika Lamb Chops

Preparation Time: 10 minutes

Cooking Time: 10 minutes

Servings: 4

Ingredients:

- ½ lb lamb racks (cut into chops)
- ¾ cup cumin powder
- 3 Tbsp paprika
- 1 tsp chili powder
- Salt and pepper, to taste

Directions:

1. Combine the paprika, cumin, chili, salt and pepper in a bowl.
2. Allow the spice mixture to cling to the lamb chops before serving.
3. Heat the grill to medium, place the lamb chops on it, and cook for 5 minutes.
4. Change the side and cook for another 5 minutes.
5. Serve and have fun.

Nutrition:

Nutritional Info (per serving)				
Calories	*Fat*	*Carbs*	*Sodium*	*Protein*
543	37 g	19 g	236 mg	109 g

74.   Healthy Sirloin Steak

Preparation Time: 10 minutes

Cooking Time: 14 minutes

Servings: 4

Ingredients:

- 1 cup mushrooms
- 1 lb boneless beef sirloin steak
- 1 large red onion (chopped)
- 4 garlic cloves (thinly sliced)
- 1 cup parsley leaves (finely cut)
- 4 Tbsp olive oil

Directions:

1. Heat only 2 Tbsp of oil in a large pot over medium-high heat.
2. Cook until the meat is browned on all sides; remove the steak from the pan and discard the fat.
3. Add the remaining oil to the skillet and heat it. Cook, often stirring, for 2–3 minutes after adding the onions and garlic. Reduce the heat to low and add the steak back to the skillet.
4. With the cover on, cook for 3-4 minutes.
5. Serve with parsley as a garnish. Serve and have fun.

Nutrition:

Nutritional Info (per serving)				
Calories	*Fat*	*Carbs*	*Sodiium*	*Protein*
854	56 g	27 g	90 mg	89 g

75.   Sweet and Sour Pork

Preparation Time: 10 minutes

Cooking Time: 12 minutes

Servings: 4

Ingredients:

- ½ lb Lean pork (cut into 1 inch cubes)
- 1 tsp olive oil
- 1 tsp ground ginger
- Black pepper, to taste
- Vegetable oil for frying

Batter:

- 1 ½ cup plain flour
- 1 ¼ cup water
- ½ tsp oil
- 1 small egg

Sweet and Sour Sauce:

- 2 Tbsp white sugar
- 6 Tbsp vinegar
- ¾ cup water
- 2 tsp cornflour (heaped)
- 2 Tbsp pineapple juice (can be drained from a tin)
- Black pepper, to taste
- A few drops red food coloring

Directions:

1. Make a well with a spoon in the center of the flour in a basin. Gradually beat in the water while adding the egg. Set aside for 20 minutes after adding the oil.
2. In a saucepan, combine the sugar, pepper, vinegar, water and pineapple juice, and bring to a boil for 2 minutes. Maintain a high temperature.
3. Combine the pork cubes, olive oil, pepper and ground ginger in a mixing dish. Mix thoroughly. Remove any extra flour from the pork after coating it in 2 Tbsp of flour.
4. In a mixing bowl, combine the meat and the batter. In a deep pot, heat the oil until it is hot but not smoking. Cook the battered pork for 8–9 minutes or until golden brown in the oil. Drain it on absorbent paper.
5. Serve in a hot serving dish with the sauce on top.

Nutrition:

Calories	Fat	Carbs	Sodium	Protein
Nutritional Info (per serving)				
1689	77 g	62 g	336 mg	188 g

76.   Easy Pork Chops

Preparation Time: 10 minutes

Cooking Time: twenty or so minutes

Servings: 4

Ingredients:

- 4 pork chops, boneless
- 1 Tbsp extra-virgin olive oil
- 1 cup chicken stock, low-sodium
- A pinch black pepper
- 1 tsp sweet paprika

Directions:

1. Heat a pan while using the oil over medium-high heat, add pork chops, brown them for 5 minutes on either side, add paprika, black pepper, and stock, and toss.
2. Cook for 15 minutes more, divide between plates, and serve by using a side salad.
3. Enjoy!

Nutrition:

Nutritional Info (per serving)				
Calories	*Fat*	*Carbs*	*Fiber*	*Protein*
654	34 g	14 g	8 g	67 g

77.   Pork Salad

Preparation Time: 10 minutes

Cooking Time: 35 minutes

Servings: 4

Ingredients:

- 1 lb pork tenderloin, cut into small slices
- 1 Tbsp lemon peel, grated
- 6 sage leaves, chopped
- A pinch black pepper
- ½ tsp cumin, ground
- 1 Tbsp organic essential olive oil
- 1 green lettuce head, torn
- 1 ½ cup tomatoes, chopped
- 1 avocado, peeled, pitted and cubed
- 1 cup canned black beans, no-salt-added, drained and rinsed
- ½ cup green onions, chopped

For the Vinaigrette:

- 1 red sweet pepper, halved
- 1 jalapeno, halved
- 2 Tbsp lime juice
- 2 Tbsp using apple cider vinegar
- 2 Tbsp organic olive oil

Directions:

1. In a bowl, combine the pork slices with lemon peel, sage, cumin and black pepper, and toss well, leaving aside to 10 minutes.
2. Heat a pan with 1 Tbsp oil over medium-high heat, add the pork slices, cook them for 5 minutes on them, and transfer them using a plate.
3. Arrange sweet pepper halves and jalapeno having a lined baking sheet, introduce in the oven, bake at 425°F for 25 minutes, cool them down, peel, and place them in your food processor.
4. Add 2 Tbsp lime juice, vinegar and a pair of Tbsp oil, and pulse well.
5. In a salad bowl, combine the lettuce with avocado, tomatoes, black beans and green onions, toss, and divide between plates.
6. Top this mix with pork slices, drizzle the vinaigrette across, and serve for lunch.
7. Enjoy!

Nutrition:

Nutritional Info (per serving)				
Calories	*Fat*	*Carbs*	*Fiber*	*Protein*
2359	86 g	67 g	88 g	188 g

78.   Lamb and Ginger Stir Fry

Preparation Time: 10 minutes

Cooking Time: 8 minutes

Servings: 2

Ingredients:

- ¾ lb minced lamb
- 1 tsp ginger root (chopped or grated)
- 1 Tbsp cooked peas
- A little sunflower oil
- Pepper, to taste

Directions:

1. Fry the lamb for 3–4 minutes in the sunflower oil or until lightly browned.
2. Add the ginger and continue to cook for another 2–3 minutes, stirring constantly.
3. Season with pepper and add the peas.

Nutrition:

Nutritional Info (per serving)				
Calories	*Fat*	*Carbs*	*Sodium*	*Protein*
786	12 g	18 g	126 mg	35 g

79.   Perfect Pulled Pork

Preparation Time: 5 hours

Cooking Time: 1 hour 30 minutes

Servings: 6

Ingredients:

- 2 lb pork shoulder joint, rind on

For the Marinade

- 1 ½ oz tomato purée (around 3 Tbsp)
- 1 oz chipotle paste (around 2 Tbsp)
- Juice 2 large oranges
- Juice 2 limes
- 1 tsp flaked sea salt
- 1 tsp ground cumin
- 1 tsp ground allspice
- 1 tsp coarsely ground black pepper

Directions:

1. In a large non-metallic mixing basin, whisk the tomato purée, chipotle paste, orange and lime juice, salt and spices to form the marinade.
2. Please remove any remaining string from the pork and place it in the marinade. Turn the pork several times until it is well coated, then cover and marinate overnight in the refrigerator.
3. Preheat the oven to 330°F. In a medium casserole, combine the pork and marinade, cover, and bake for 3 hours, or until the pork breaks apart when probed with a fork.
4. After a couple of hours, check the pork and add a little more water if necessary to keep it moist.
5. Shred the pork with forks on a board or hot dish, discarding the rind and fat.
6. Serve with a spoonful of the spicy cooking liquid on top.

Nutrition:

Nutritional Info (per serving)				
Calories	*Fat*	*Carbs*	*Sodium*	*Protein*
919	55 g	63 g	262 mg	148 g

80.   Roasted Beef and Pepperoncini

Preparation Time: 2 hours 10 minutes

Cooking Time: 30 minutes

Servings: 4

Ingredients:

- 2 Tbsp melted ghee
- 1 cup veggie stock
- 1 Tbsp coconut aminos
- 2 lb beef chuck roast
- 10 pepperoncini

Directions:

1. Prepare the baking tray with some greasing.
2. Set on the baking tray the meat, pepperoncini, stock and aminos, then cover.
3. Set the oven for 2 hours at 375°F, and allow it to bake.
4. Set the meat on a chopping board to slice and serve topped with the pepperoncini mix.
5. Enjoy.

Nutrition:

Nutritional Info (per serving)				
Calories	*Fat*	*Carbs*	*Fiber*	*Protein*
1678	61 g	23 g	8 g	127 g

81.   Spicy Grainy Lamb

Preparation Time: 10 minutes

Cooking Time: 35 minutes plus 10 minutes resting

Servings: 10

Ingredients:

- ¼ cup whole-grain Dijon mustard
- 1 Tbsp fresh rosemary, chopped
- 2 Tbsp fresh thyme, chopped
- Ground black pepper
- Sea salt
- 1 Tbsp olive oil
- 2 (8-rib) frenched lamb racks, patted dry

Directions:

1. Preheat the oven to 425°F (220ºC).
2. In a bowl, stir well the mustard, rosemary and thyme.
3. Season the lamb racks with pepper and sea salt.
4. Arrange an ovenproof skillet over medium-high heat and pour the olive oil.
5. Add the lamb racks. Pan-sear for about 2 minutes per side. Remove the skillet from the heat.
6. Turn the racks upright in the skillet with the bones interlaced and spread the mustard mixture over the outside surface of the lamb; roast for about 30 minutes.
7. Remove the lamb racks from the oven and set aside for about 10 minutes.
8. Cut the racks into chops.
9. Enjoy.

Nutrition:

Nutritional Info (per serving)				
Calories	Fat	Carbs	Fiber	Protein
676	21 g	12 g	0 g	65 g

82.   Rosemary Lamb Bowls

Preparation Time: 30 minutes

Cooking Time: 4 hours

Servings: 4

Ingredients:

- 2 chopped carrots
- Rosemary sprigs at will
- 1 cup beef stock
- 2 lb cubed lamb
- 1 tomato, chopped
- 2 Tbsp ghee

- 1 tsp chopped thyme
- 1 garlic cloves
- 1 yellow onion, chopped
- 1 cup White wine
- Salt and black pepper

Directions:

1. Pour oil into the Dutch oven over medium-high heat and brown the beef seasoned with salt and pepper on all sides and set aside.
2. Add in the onions to fry for 2 minutes.
3. Mix in the garlic, wine, rosemary, thyme, carrots, salt, pepper and tomatoes, and cook for some minutes.
4. Mix in the lamb and turn down the heat to medium-low. Close and cook for 4 hours.
5. Season with salt and pepper, and remove the sprigs.
6. Serve in bowls.

Nutrition:

Nutritional Info (per serving)				
Calories	*Fat*	*Carbs*	*Fiber*	*Protein*
970	53 g	60 g	6 g	67 g

83.   Sauerkraut Soup and Beef

Preparation Time: 1 hour and 30 minutes

Cooking Time: 30 minutes

Servings: 4

Ingredients:

- 1 lb ground beef
- 3 Tbsp chopped fresh parsley
- 1 onion (peeled and chopped)
- 1 tsp dried sage
- 3 tsp olive oil
- 14 oz beef stock
- 2 cups chicken stock
- 14 oz canned tomatoes and juice
- 1 Tbsp gluten-free Worcestershire sauce
- 4 bay leaves
- 1 Tbsp garlic (minced)
- 2 cups water
- 1 Tbsp Stevia
- 14 oz chopped sauerkraut
- Seasoning: Salt and ground black pepper

Directions:

1. Heat 1 tsp of oil in a pan at medium temperature, put the beef, stir properly, and brown for 10 minutes.
2. Mix chicken stock, beef stock, sauerkraut, stevia, canned tomatoes, Worcestershire sauce, parsley, sage, and bay leaves in a pot, and cool slowly, bring to simmer with medium heat.
3. Put the beef into the soup, mix well, and continue to cook slowly.
4. Pour the remaining oil into a pan and heat at medium temperature, Supplement with onions, mix well, and cook for 2 more minutes.
5. Also, put garlic, stir cook for 1 minute, and pour into the soup.
6. Reduce the heat for the soup and cook slowly for 1 hour.
7. Mix salt, pepper, and water carefully and cook for 15 minutes.
8. Divide between bowls and serve it.

Nutrition:

Nutritional Info (per serving)				
Calories	Fat	Carbs	Fiber	Protein
1198	47 g	116 g	5 g	119 g

84.   Seared Beef Soup Bowls

Preparation Time: 4 hours 20 minutes

Cooking Time: 30 minutes

Servings: 4

Ingredients:

- 2 lb cubed beef
- 4 Thyme sprigs
- 8 oz chopped pancetta
- Chopped parsley at will
- 2 Tbsp Ghee
- 3 lemon peel strips
- 2 Tbsp Tomato paste

- 2 Tbsp Olive oil
- 2 cinnamon sticks
- 4 minced garlic cloves
- 2 chopped brown onions
- 4 Tbsp red vinegar
- 4 cups beef stock
- Salt and black pepper

Directions:

1. Put pancetta, garlic, oil and onion in a pan over medium-high and fry for 5 minutes.
2. Add the beef cubes to brown, then mix in the salt, pepper, vinegar, cinnamon, lemon peel, tomato paste, ghee and thyme, and cook for 3 minutes.
3. Put everything in a crock pot and cook for 4 hours on high.
4. Remove the thyme, lemon peel and cinnamon and mix in the parsley.
5. Serve.

Nutrition:

Nutritional Info (per serving)				
Calories	Fat	Carbs	Fiber	Protein
991	36 g	27 g	1 g	93 g

85.   Seared Beef with Peanut Sauce

Preparation Time: 20 minutes

Cooking Time: 30 minutes

Servings: 4

Ingredients:

- 1 cup beef stock
- 3 green onions, chopped
- 1 lb beef steak, cut into strips
- 1 green bell pepper, chopped
- 1 ½ tsp lemon pepper
- 1 Tbsp coconut aminos
- 4 Tbsp peanut butter
- ¼ tsp onion powder
- ¼ tsp garlic powder
- Salt
- Pepper

Directions:

1. Combine lemon pepper, stock, peanut butter and coconut aminos together in a bowl and set aside.
2. Sprinkle the beef with salt, onion powder, garlic powder and pepper, and sear it on a pan over medium-high for 7 minutes.
3. Mix in the green pepper and let it cook for 3 minutes.
4. Add in the green onions and the peanut sauce and let it cook for 1 minute.
5. Serve.

Nutrition:

Nutritional Info (per serving)				
Calories	*Fat*	*Carbs*	*Fiber*	*Protein*
1123	65 g	72 g	1 g	159 g

86.   Seared Veal and Capers

Preparation Time: 25 minutes

Cooking Time: 30 minutes

Servings: 2

Ingredients:

- 8 oz Veal scallops
- 1 ½ Tbsp capers
- 2 Tbsp butter
- ¼ cup chicken stock
- 1 minced garlic clove
- ¼ cup white wine
- Salt and ground black pepper.

Directions:

1. Dissolve the butter in a pan on medium-high.
2. Sprinkle salt and pepper on the veal and brown each side for 1 minute. Set aside
3. On medium, add garlic to the pan and cook for 1 minute.
4. Pour in the wine and let it boil for 2 minutes.
5. Pour in stock, butter, capers, pepper and salt, and then add the veal to the broth, and mix well.
6. Close the pan and cook until the veal is soft.

Nutrition:

Nutritional Info (per serving)				
Calories	Fat	Carbs	Fiber	Protein
876	21 g	126 g	8 g	59 g

Chapter #6: Main Dishes: Fish and Seafood

87.   Shrimp and Calamari with Avocado Sauce

Preparation Time: 35 minutes

Cooking Time: 30 minutes   **Servings:** 1

Ingredients:

- 1 egg
- 1 Tbsp coconut oil
- 1 tsp tomato paste
- 8 oz calamari, sliced into medium rings
- 1 Tbsp mayonnaise
- 1 tsp lemon juice
- 3 Tbsp coconut flour

- 2 Tbsp avocado, cored and diced
- A splash Worcestershire sauce
- 2 lemon slices
- Salt and black pepper ground, to taste
- 7 oz shrimp, peeled and deveined
- ½ Tsp turmeric

Directions:

1. Whisk the egg with coconut oil in a medium-sized bowl.
2. Dip the calamari rings and shrimp in the egg mixture and coat them well.
3. Combine the flour with turmeric, pepper and salt in another shallow bowl.
4. Place the shrimp and calamari rings in the dry flour mixture.
5. Coat them well and shake off the excess flour.
6. Place the coated shrimp and calamari rings on a greased baking sheet
7. Bake the seafood for 10 minutes at 400°F in a preheated oven.
8. Remove the baking sheet from the oven and flip all the shrimp and rings.
9. Continue baking them for another 10 minutes.
10. Meanwhile, mash the avocado flesh in a glass bowl.
11. Stir in mayonnaise, tomato paste, lemon juice, salt, pepper and Worcestershire sauce. Mix well.
12. Divide the baked shrimp and calamari into the serving plates.
13. Serve them with avocado sauce and lemon slice. Enjoy.

Nutrition:

Nutritional Info (per serving)				
Calories	*Fat*	*Carbs*	*Fiber*	*Protein*
2016	61 g	126 g	2 g	163 g

88.   Simple Baked Catfish with Salad

Preparation Time: 30 minutes

Cooking Time: 30 minutes

Servings: 4

Ingredients:

- 2 Tbsp parsley, chopped
- ½ tsp basil, dried
- ½ tsp thyme, dried
- ½ tsp oregano, dried
- 1 tsp sweet paprika
- A pinch salt and black pepper
- 4 medium catfish fillets, boneless
- 4 lemon juice
- ¼ tsp garlic powder
- 2 Tbsp ghee, melted

Directions:

1. Pour some melted ghee into a baking dish to act as grease and place the fish fillets neatly in the dish.
2. Then add parsley, basil, thyme, oregano, paprika, salt, pepper, lemon juice and the garlic powder.
3. Toss gently to make sure it is properly coated, then move into an oven and bake at 350°F for about 20 minutes.
4. Divide the fish into different plates
5. Serve with a side salad
6. Enjoy.

Nutrition:

Nutritional Info (per serving)				
Calories	Fat	Carbs	Fiber	Protein
655	8 g	30 g	3 g	57 g

89.   Simple Sardines and Cucumber Mix

Preparation Time: 10 minutes

Cooking Time: 30 minutes

Servings: 2

Ingredients:

- 10 oz canned sardines in oil, cubed.
- 2 Tbsp lemon juice
- 2 small cucumbers, chopped
- 1 Tbsp mustard
- Salt and black pepper, to taste

Directions:

1. Mix the sardines with a pinch of salt, pepper, cucumber, lemon juice and mustard in a clean bowl.
2. Then stir gently and serve.
3. Enjoy!

Nutrition:

Nutritional Info (per serving)				
Calories	Fat	Carbs	Fiber	Protein
476	10 g	50 g	4 g	43 g

90.   Steak Tuna

Preparation Time: 35 minutes

Cooking Time: 50 minutes

Servings: 1

Ingredients:

- ¼ lb fresh tuna steak, cut into roughly 1 inch chunks
- 1 Tbsp coconut or rapeseed oil
- 12 oz pack stir-fry vegetables
- 2 Tbsp ready-made hoisin sauce
- Pinch crushed dried chili
- Salt and black pepper, to taste

Directions:

1. Sprinkle salt and black pepper on the tuna.
2. Heat the oil in a large nonstick frying pan or wok over high heat and stir-fry the tuna and veggies for 3–4 minutes, or until the tuna is gently browned, or according to the package directions.
3. Drizzle the hoisin sauce over the fish and veggies and toss for another 20–30 seconds.
4. If using, top with the chili flakes and serve right away.

Nutrition:

Nutritional Info (per serving)				
Calories	Fat	Carbs	Sodium	Protein
789	15 g	76 g	224 mg	35 g

91.   Shrimp Fajita

Preparation Time: 10 minutes

Cooking Time: 10 minutes

Servings: 4

Ingredients:

- 1 small onion, thinly sliced
- 1 lb shrimp, deveined
- 2 tsp chili powder
- 1 (red) bell pepper, thinly sliced
- 1 (orange) bell pepper, thinly sliced
- 1 (yellow) bell pepper, thinly sliced
- ½ tsp onion powder
- ½ tsp cumin, ground
- 1 tsp kosher salt
- 1 ½ Tbsp olive oil, extra-virgin
- ½ tsp garlic powder
- ½ tsp smoked paprika
- Freshly ground pepper, to taste
- Cilantro for garnish
- Lime for garnish

Directions:

1. Set the oven temperature to 450°F.
2. In a sizable mixing basin, combine the onion, bell pepper, shrimp, olive oil, pepper, salt and spices.
3. Combine all the ingredients.
4. Coat the baking sheet with nonstick cooking spray.
5. Arrange the shrimp, bell peppers and onions on a baking pan.
6. Cook at 450°F for around 8 to 10 minutes. Set the oven to broil and heat for 1 to 2 minutes or until the shrimp is completely cooked.
7. Serve with fresh cilantro sprinkled on top and fresh lime juice drizzled over the fajita mixture.

Nutrition:

Nutritional Info (per serving)				
Calories	*Fat*	*Carbs*	*Fiber*	*Protein*
1837	69 g	135 g	0 g	82 g

92.   Salmon and Salsa

Preparation Time: 15 minutes

Cooking Time: 10 minutes

Servings: 4

Ingredients:

- 4 medium salmon fillets, boneless
- 2 tsp olive oil
- 4 tsp lemon juice
- 1 garlic clove, minced
- 1 tsp sweet paprika
- A pinch salt and black pepper

For the Salsa:

- ¼ cup chopped green onions
- 1 cup chopped red bell pepper
- 4 tsp chopped oregano
- 1 small habanero pepper, chopped
- 1 garlic clove, minced
- ¼ cup lemon juice

Directions:

1. In a bowl, mix the red bell pepper with habanero, green onion, ¼ cup lemon juice, 1 garlic clove, oregano, salt and black pepper.
2. In a separate large bowl, mix paprika, olive oil, 1 garlic clove and 4 tsp of lemon juice. Stir, add the fish, rub it with the seasoning mix, and leave aside for 10 minutes.
3. Put the fish on the preheated grill over medium-high heat, season with sea salt and black pepper, then cook for 5 minutes on each side.
4. Divide between plates, top with the salsa, and serve. Enjoy!

Nutrition:

Nutritional Info (per serving)				
Calories	Fat	Carbs	Fiber	Protein
959	57 g	63 g	2 g	48 g

93. Wrapped Salmon

Preparation Time: 10 minutes

Cooking Time: 20 minutes

Servings: 4

Ingredients:

- 6 cabbage leaves, sliced in half
- 4 medium salmon steaks, skinless
- 2 red bell peppers, chopped
- 2 Tbsp coconut oil
- 1 yellow onion, chopped
- A pinch sea salt and black pepper

Directions:

1. Put some water in a pot, bring to a boil over medium-high heat, add the cabbage leaves and blanch them for 2 minutes, then transfer them to a bowl filled with cold water to stop the cooking.
2. Remove from the water and pat them dry, then set aside. Season the salmon steaks with salt and black pepper to the taste and wrap each in 3 cabbage leaf halves.
3. Heat a pan with the coconut oil over medium-high heat, add onion and bell pepper, stir, and cook for 4 minutes. Add the wrapped salmon and place the pan in the oven at 350°F. Bake for 12 minutes.
4. Divide the wrapped salmon and veggies between plates and serve.
5. Enjoy!

Nutrition:

Nutritional Info (per serving)				
Calories	*Fat*	*Carbs*	*Fiber*	*Protein*
890	**48 g**	**92 g**	**5 g**	**48 g**

94.   Sesame Salmon with Broccoli and Tomatoes

Preparation Time: 30 minutes

Cooking Time: 25 minutes

Servings: 2

Ingredients:

- 2 tsp rapeseed oil
- 2 pieces salmon fillets
- 6 spring onions
- 12 tomatoes
- 1 cup broccoli, trimmed
- 1 Tbsp soya sauce
- Ground black pepper, to taste
- 1 tsp Sesame oil
- ½ tsp crushed dried chili flakes
- 1 tsp sesame seeds

Directions:

1. Preheat the oven to 400°F. Drizzle the oil over a baking tray.
2. Place the salmon fillets down in the tray, along with the spring onions and tomatoes, and season generously with ground black pepper.
3. Heat the oven to 350°F and bake for 8 minutes. In the meantime, fill a pan halfway with water and bring it to a boil.
4. Return the pot to a boil with the broccoli. Drain after 4 minutes of cooking. Place the broccoli on the baking tray after removing it from the oven.
5. Soya sauce and sesame oil should be drizzled over the fish. Revert the salmon to the oven for the next 3 to 4 minutes, or until just done, then sprinkle with the chili powder and sesame seeds.
6. Split it up between 2 heated plates to serve.

Nutrition:

Nutritional Info (per serving)				
Calories	*Fat*	*Carbs*	*Fiber*	*Protein*
587	38 g	61 g	38 g	35 g

95.   Thai Curry with Prawns

Preparation Time: 20 minutes

Cooking Time: 30 minutes

Servings: 2

Ingredients:

- 1 Tbsp coconut oil
- 1 red pepper cut into roughly 4/5-inch chunks
- 4 spring onions thickly sliced
- 1 oz root ginger, peeled and finely grated
- 3 Tbsp Thai red curry paste
- 1 ½ cup coconut milk (about ½ can)
- ½ cup mangetout or sugar snap peas, halved
- 1 red chili, finely sliced
- ½ lb cooked prawns

Directions:

1. Take a large nonstick frying pan, heat the oil over medium-high heat, and stir-fry the pepper for 2 minutes. Cook for another minute, constantly stirring, after adding the spring onions, ginger and curry paste.
2. Fill the pan halfway with coconut milk and bring to a medium simmer. Add the mange tout or sugar snap peas and the chili if using.
3. Return to low heat and cook for another 2 minutes, stirring occasionally. Heat for 1–2 minutes or until the prawns are heated.
4. If the sauce becomes thick, too, add a drop of water.
5. Serve with cauliflower rice that has just been cooked.

Nutrition:

Calories	Fat	Carbs	Sodium	Protein
589	43 g	48 g	352 mg	19 g

Nutritional Info (per serving)

96.   Mussels with Creamy Tarragon Sauce

Preparation Time: 20 minutes

Cooking Time: 25 minutes

Servings: 4

Ingredients:

- 2 ¼ lb fresh, live mussels
- 1 Tbsp olive oil
- 1 medium leek, trimmed and thinly sliced (around 3 ½ oz prepared weight)
- 2 garlic cloves, peeled and thinly sliced
- ½ cup dry white wine
- 3 Tbsp full-Protein crème fraiche
- 3–4 fresh tarragon stalks (around 1 tsp), leaves picked and roughly chopped or 1 tsp dried tarragon

Directions:

1. Remove the 'beards' by dumping the mussels into the sink and scrubbing them thoroughly under cold running water.
2. Mussels with broken shells or that do not close when struck on the side of the sink should be discarded. Drain the ones that are good in a colander.
3. Heat the oil over low heat in a deep, lidded, wide-based saucepan or shallow casserole. Gently sauté the leek and garlic for 2–3 minutes, or until softened but not browned.
4. Season generously with salt and pepper after adding the white wine, crème Fraiche and tarragon.
5. Bring the wine to a simmer by increasing the heat under the pan. Cook for about 4 minutes, or until most of the mussels have steamed open after stirring in the mussels and covering closely with a lid. Stir thoroughly, then cover and cook for another 1–2 minutes, or until the rest of the vegetables are done.
6. Remove any mussels that haven't opened, divide the mussels between 2 bowls, and pour the tarragon broth over the top.

Nutrition:

Calories	Fat	Carbs	Sodium	Protein
1327	112 g	48 g	1 g	97 g

97.   Prawn Nasi Goreng

Preparation Time: 20 minutes

Cooking Time: 35 minutes

Servings: 2

Ingredients:

- 2 Tbsp coconut
- 1 medium onion, peeled and diced
- 1 red pepper cut into roughly 4/5-inch chunks
- ½ small Savoy cabbage leaves thinly sliced
- 2 garlic cloves, peeled and thinly sliced
- 1 Tbsp root ginger, peeled and finely grated
- ½–1 tsp crushed dried chili flakes
- 7 oz cauliflower rice
- 2 Tbsp soya sauce
- 1 ½ cup prawns
- Generous handful fresh coriander leaves roughly chopped
- 1 Tbsp roasted peanuts, roughly chopped

Directions:

1. Take a large nonstick frying pan or wok, and heat the oil over medium-high heat.
2. For 2–3 minutes, stirring constantly, stir-fry the onion, red pepper and cabbage. Stir in the garlic, ginger, chili and cauliflower rice for another 2–3 minutes, or until the cauliflower is heated through.
3. Cook for another 1–2 minutes, swirling and tossing until the prawns are heated, before adding the soy sauce, prawns and half of the coriander if using.
4. To taste: Add extra soy sauce.
5. If using, top with the chopped nuts and the leftover coriander, and divide between bowls.

Nutrition:

Calories	Fat	Carbs	Sodium	Protein
761	21 g	93 g	86 mg	69 g

98.   Baked Salmon with Pea and Broccoli Mash

Preparation Time: 30 minutes

Cooking Time: 35 minutes

Servings: 2

Ingredients:

- 1 Tbsp butter, plus extra for greasing
- ½ lb fresh salmon fillets
- ¾ cup frozen peas
- 2 cups broccoli cut into small florets and stalks thinly sliced
- 1 Tbsp finely chopped fresh mint (optional)
- Lemon wedges to serve
- Salt and ground black pepper, to taste

Directions:

1. Preheat the oven to 392°F.
2. Line a small baking pan and lightly coat it with butter using foil. Season the salmon with a bit of salt and some ground black pepper and place it skin-side down on the foil. Depending on thickness, bake for 10–12 minutes.
3. On the other hand, half-fill a pan with water and boil it to prepare the pea and broccoli mash. Return the pot to a boil with the peas and broccoli. Cook, occasionally stirring, for 5 minutes or until the broccoli is cooked.
4. Wash the veggies and return them to the pan with a tiny ladleful of cooking water (about 1/3 cup). Stir with a stick blender until almost smooth, adding the butter, mint if using and 3 Tbsp of the conserved cooking water.
5. Season to taste and loosen with a splash of water if necessary. Split the mash among 2 heated plates and top with the seared salmon, which you can simply break open from the foil and discard.
6. Serve with a lemon wedge.

Nutrition:

Nutritional Info (per serving)				
Calories	*Fat*	*Carbs*	*Sodium*	*Protein*
652	37 g	61 g	96 mg	47 g

99.   Smoked Salmon with Eggs Salad

Preparation Time: 6 minutes

Cooking Time: 30 minutes

Servings: 4

Ingredients:

- 6 Eggs, hard-boiled, peeled and mashed with a fork
- 8 oz smoked salmon, cubed
- Salt and black pepper, to taste
- 1 yellow onion, chopped
- ¾ cup avocado mayonnaise

Directions:

1. Pour the eggs with mayo, salmon, salt, pepper and onion into a clean bowl and mix together.
2. Toss to make sure it is well coated.
3. Then divide into different small cups and serve.
4. Enjoy!

Nutrition:

Nutritional Info (per serving)				
Calories	*Fat*	*Carbs*	*Fiber*	*Protein*
963	78 g	91 g	23 g	86 g

100.   Shrimp Skewers with Mango Cucumber Salsa

Preparation Time: 10 minutes + 30 minutes to marinate

Cooking Time: 15 minutes

Servings: 6

Ingredients:

For Shrimp:

- Juice 2 limes
- 2 Tbsp honey
- 1 tsp canola oil
- 1 inch piece ginger (minced)
- 1 lb large shrimp

For Salsa:

- ¼ cup diced sweet onion
- 1 small red chili (finely diced)
- Juice 1 lime
- 1 medium cucumber (seeded and diced)
- 1 mango (peeled and diced)

Directions:

1. Combine the lime juice, honey and ginger in a medium mixing basin. Toss in the shrimp to coat them. To marinate, cover and chill for 30 minutes.
2. Using skewers, thread the shrimp onto the skewers. Brush a grill with oil and heat over medium-high heat.
3. Cook the skewers for 3 to 6 minutes on each side, or until the shrimp are opaque and done.

For salsa:

1. Toss the onion, chili, cucumber, mango and lime juice in a small bowl. Toss in the shrimp to coat them.

Nutrition:

Nutritional Info (per serving)				
Calories	*Fat*	*Carbs*	*Sodium*	*Protein*
907	23 g	30 g	225 mg	52 g

101.   Shrimp and Bok Choy in Parchment

Preparation Time: 10 minutes

Cooking Time: 15 minutes

Servings: 4

Ingredients:

- 12 oz shrimp (peeled and deveined)
- 3 garlic cloves (minced)
- 1 tsp toasted sesame oil
- 2 Tbsp rice vinegar
- 2 tsp honey
- 2 Tbsp freshly squeezed lime juice
- 1 lb choy (white and green parts thinly sliced)
- 2 scallions (thinly sliced)
- 2 inches piece ginger (minced)
- 1 jalapeño pepper (thinly sliced)
- ¼ cup chopped cilantro

Directions:

1. Preheat the oven to 375°F.
2. Combine the shrimp, garlic and ginger in a small bowl. Combine the sesame oil, honey, lime juice and rice vinegar in a separate small bowl.
3. Cut 4 huge circles out of parchment paper, each about 12 inches in diameter. Place a large bunch of choy on each piece, then top with the shrimp, garlic-ginger mixture, scallions and jalapeno slices. Drizzle one-quarter of the vinegar–lime juice mixture over each mound.
4. To make a half-moon shape, fold the parchment paper in half. To make a seal, fold the edges together.
5. Cook the packets for 15 minutes on a rimmed baking sheet.
6. Before serving, remove the pan from the oven and set it aside for 5 minutes. Keep an eye out for leaking steam while opening the package.
7. Serve with white rice and cilantro as a garnish.

Nutrition:

Nutritional Info (per serving)				
Calories	*Fat*	*Carbs*	*Sodium*	*Protein*
1630	43 g	27 g	193 mg	91 g

102. Shrimp Fried Rice

Preparation Time: 10 minutes

Cooking Time: 15 minutes

Servings: 6

Ingredients:

- 1 Tbsp extra-virgin olive oil
- ½ sweet onion (chopped)
- 1 cup sugar snap peas
- 2 inches piece ginger (minced)
- 3 garlic cloves (minced)
- 1 lb shrimp (peeled and deveined)
- 3 cups cooked rice

Directions:

1. Warm the oil in a pot over medium-high heat. Cook, constantly stirring, for 3 to 5 minutes or until the onion softens. Stir in the ginger and garlic until they are fragrant.
2. Cook the shrimp, often tossing, for approximately 5 minutes or until the shrimp is opaque and almost cooked through. Stir in the snap peas and rice until well combined and heated. Serve.

Nutrition:

Calories	Fat	Carbs	Sodium	Protein
Nutritional Info (per serving)				
1161	37 g	77 g	266 g	63 g

103. Creamy Shrimp Fettuccine

Preparation Time: 10 minutes

Cooking Time: 30 minutes

Servings: 4

Ingredients:

- 8 oz dried fettuccine
- 3 garlic cloves (minced)
- 2 Tbsp extra-virgin olive oil (divided)
- 10 oz shrimp (peeled and deveined)
- 1 cup Homemade Rice Milk or unsweetened store-bought rice milk
- 1 tsp garlic powder
- 2 Tbsp all-purpose flour
- ¼ cup grated Parmesan cheese
- 2 Tbsp chopped parsley
- Lemon, cut into wedges (for serving)
- Freshly ground black pepper

Directions:

1. A large stockpot of salted water should be brought to a boil. Add the fettuccine and simmer, turning regularly, until the noodles are al dente. Drain.
2. Add 1 Tbsp olive oil and heat it in a large pan over medium heat. Cook the shrimp, stirring periodically, for 3 to 5 minutes, or until the shrimp are pink and opaque. Remove the shrimp from the pan in the same skillet, and add the remaining Tbsp of oil. Constantly stir until the garlic is fragrant.
3. Combine the flour and water, and stir until the paste forms. Slowly drizzle in the rice milk, a little at a time, constantly whisking until the mixture is smooth. Add the garlic powder and mix well. Slow down the heat to low and cook until the sauce thickens.
4. Add the Parmesan cheese and mix well. Season with salt and pepper. Toss in the noodles and toss well to coat. Add the shrimp and mix well.
5. Serve with lemon wedges and parsley on the side.

Nutrition:

Nutritional Info (per serving)				
Calories	*Fat*	*Carbs*	*Sodium*	*Protein*
1127	72 g	272 g	136 mg	37 g

104. White Fish and Broccoli Curry

Preparation Time: 10 minutes

Cooking Time: 10 minutes

Servings: 6

Ingredients:

For Curry Paste:

- ½ sweet onion, chopped
- 1 medium red chili, chopped
- 1 tsp turmeric powder
- 1-inch piece ginger, peeled and chopped
- ½ tsp cumin seeds
- 1 lemongrass stalk (outer leaves removed, tender bottom portion, chopped)
- ¼ cup roughly chopped fresh cilantro stems
- 2 Tbsp extra-virgin olive oil

For Curry:

- ¾ cup Homemade Rice Milk/unsweetened store-bought rice milk
- ½ cup cream cheese
- 3 cups broccoli florets
- 1 lb tilapia fillets
- Juice 1 lime
- 1 tsp sugar

Directions:

For Curry Paste:

1. Combine the onion, chili, ginger, lemongrass, cilantro, turmeric, cumin seeds and olive oil in a mortar and pestle or blender, and mix until smooth.

For Curry:

1. Heat the curry paste in a large pan over medium-high heat for 2 to 3 minutes, stirring periodically, until aromatic.

2. Stir in the rice milk until it is completely mixed. Bring to a low boil, then reduce to low heat. Meanwhile, place the cream cheese.
3. Stir in a few Tbsp of the heated rice-milk mixture until smooth. Add the tilapia and broccoli to the pan, then gently whisk in the cream cheese mixture to combine.
4. Cook till the fish is perfectly cooked, the broccoli is tender, and the curry is bubbling. Combine the lime juice and sugar in a mixing bowl.
5. Take the pan off the heat and serve over white rice.

Nutrition:

Nutritional Info (per serving)				
Calories	Fat	Carbs	Sodium	Protein
1273	61 g	232 g	266 g	26 g

105.   Oven-Fried Fish with Pineapple Salsa

Preparation Time: 10 minutes

Cooking Time: 20 minutes

Servings: 4

Ingredients:

For Salsa:

- 1 cup diced pineapple
- ½ jalapeño pepper (seeded and diced)
- Juice ½ lime
- ¼ cup diced red onion
- ¼ cup chopped fresh cilantro

For Fish:

- 1 Tbsp butter
- 1 lb white fish fillets

- ½ tsp garlic powder
- ¼ cup yellow cornmeal
- ¼ cup all-purpose flour
- 1 egg (beaten)
- ½ tsp paprika
- 2 Tbsp Homemade Rice Milk/unsweetened store-bought rice milk

Directions:

1. Combine the pineapple, onion, jalapeno, lime juice and cilantro in a small bowl. While you prepare the fish, toss the salad and put it aside.

For Fish:

1. Preheat the oven to 400°F.
2. Using butter, grease a small baking dish. Garlic powder and paprika are used to season the fish fillets.
3. Combine the cornmeal and flour. Combine the egg and rice milk in a separate small bowl. Each fish should be dipped in the egg mixture and then rolled into the flour mixture.
4. In the preheated pan, arrange the fish in a single layer.
5. Bake for 20 minutes or until the fish is golden brown and easily flaked with a fork.

Nutrition:

Calories	Fat	Carbs	Sodium	Protein
Nutritional Info (per serving)				
1246	35 g	212 g	270 mg	127 g

106.   Salmon and Kale in Parchment

Preparation Time: 10 minutes

Cooking Time: 15 minutes

Servings: 4

Ingredients:

- 2 cups thinly sliced kale leaves
- 2 small zucchini, sliced
- 1 lb salmon fillets
- 4 fresh thyme sprigs
- ½ tsp paprika
- 4 fresh rosemary sprigs
- 1 lemon (sliced)
- ¼ cup dry white wine
- Freshly ground black pepper as required

Directions:

1. Preheat the oven to 450°F.
2. Cut 4 pieces of parchment paper with a diameter of approximately 12 inches each. Place 2 cups of kale leaves, topped with many slices of zucchini. Season with salt and pepper.
3. Season the salmon fillets with paprika, then garnish with a sprig of thyme, a sprig of rosemary, and a slice of lemon. Pour 1 tablespoon of white wine over each fillet to seal the seams, fold the parchment paper over and wrinkle the edges. Cook for 15 minutes in the oven.
4. Remove the fillets from the oven and set them aside to cool for 5 minutes before serving.

Nutrition:

Nutritional Info (per serving)				
Calories	*Fat*	*Carbs*	*Sodium*	*Protein*
935	72 g	73 g	206 mg	165 g

107.   Salmon Burgers

Preparation Time: 10 minutes

Cooking Time: 10 minutes

Servings: 4

Ingredients:

- 1 lb salmon
- 1 Tbsp mustard
- Zest 1 lemon
- 1 Tbsp lemon juice
- 2 scallions
- ½ cup coarse bread crumbs
- 1 Tbsp extra-virgin olive oil
- Buns or greens
- Black pepper as required

Directions:

1. Remove any pin bones from the fish and chop them into slices. Add half of the salmon to a food processor and pulse until pasty. Mix mustard, lemon zest and lemon juice. Add salt and pepper.
2. Fill a bowl halfway with the fish mixture. Add the scallions and ¼ cup of bread crumbs and mix well. Make four patties out of the mixture.
3. Spread the remaining bread crumbs on a dish and gently cover each burger. Heat the olive oil in a large pan over medium-high heat. Cook the burgers.
4. Serve with a green salad, such as Mixed Green Leaf and Citrus Salad or Spinach Salad with Orange Vinaigrette, on a bun or over a bed of greens.

Nutrition:

Nutritional Info (per serving)				
Calories	*Fat*	*Carbs*	*Sodium*	*Protein*
886	52 g	112 g	256 mg	187 g

108.   Roasted Salmon with Herb Gremolata

Preparation Time: 10 minutes

Cooking Time: 15 minutes

Servings: 4

Ingredients:

- ½ cup Parsley
- Juice 1 lemon
- 2 garlic cloves
- 1 Tbsp thyme
- 1 Tbsp rosemary
- 1 lb salmon fillets
- Lemon Zest at will
- Salt and black pepper, to taste

Directions:

1. Preheat the oven to 400°F.
2. In a separate bowl, incorporate the parsley, lemon zest, lemon juice, garlic, rosemary, and thyme.
3. Stir the ingredients together to mix them. After pushing the fillets into the herb mixture to coat one side, place them herb-side up on a baking pan.
4. Season with salt and pepper to taste. Cook for 8 minutes, or when a fork easily penetrates the salmon.

Nutrition:

Nutritional Info (per serving)				
Calories	Fat	Carbs	Sodium	Protein
657	82 g	61 g	136 g	112 g

109.   Spicy Salmon Fillets with Salad

Preparation Time: 20 minutes

Cooking Time: 10 minutes

Servings: 4

Ingredients:

- 4 salmon fillets, boneless and skin-on
- 2 Tbsp chili pepper, chopped
- 1 Juice lemon
- 2 Tbsp olive oil
- A pinch salt and black pepper

Directions:

1. Place a pan containing oil over a medium-high heat source, and add chili pepper. Stir gently and cook between 1–2 minutes.
2. Add the salmon, salt and pepper, cooking each side for about 3 minutes.
3. Divide into different plates, then drizzle the lemon juice all over
4. Serve with salad on the side.
5. Enjoy your meal!

Nutrition:

Nutritional Info (per serving)				
Calories	*Fat*	*Carbs*	*Fiber*	*Protein*
636	48 g	32 g	8 g	78 g

110.   Tangy Pepper Filled Oysters

Preparation Time: 5 minutes

Cooking Time: 15 minutes

Servings: 4

Ingredients:

- ¼ cup olive oil
- 1 Serrano chili pepper, chopped
- 12 oysters, shucked
- Juice from 1 lime
- ½ tsp fresh ginger, shredded
- Juice 2 lemons
- ¼ tsp garlic, minced
- Zest from 2 limes
- ¼ cup scallions, chopped
- 1 cup tomato juice
- Salt, to taste
- ¼ cup fresh cilantro, chopped

Directions:

1. Arrange all the oysters in a baking tray with their shell side downward.
2. Mix garlic, scallions, salt, olive oil, tomato juice, serrano chili, lime juice and zest, lemon juice and zest, ginger and cilantro in a medium bowl.
3. Top each oyster with a scoop of this mixture.
4. Serve fresh.

Nutrition:

Nutritional Info (per serving)				
Calories	*Fat*	*Carbs*	*Fiber*	*Protein*
479	26 g	57 g	12 g	19 g

111.   Grilled Salmon and Asparagus Foil Packets

Preparation Time: 10 minutes

Cooking Time: 20 minutes

Servings: 4

Ingredients:

- 4 Tbsp avocado oil, divided
- 16 asparagus spears, tough ends trimmed
- 4 skinless salmon fillets
- ½ tsp salt, divided
- 1 tsp garlic powder, divided
- Freshly ground black pepper
- 1 lemon, thinly sliced

Directions:

1. Preheat the oven to 400°F (205°C).
2. On a work surface, place 4 (12-inch) squares of parchment paper or foil.
3. In the center of each square, pace with 1 salmon fillet, then add 4 asparagus spears next to each fillet. Use 1 Tbsp of avocado oil to brush the fish and asparagus.
4. Sprinkle ¼ tsp garlic powder and ⅛ tsp salt over each fillet, and season with pepper.
5. On top of the fillets cover with the lemon slices. Close and seal the parchment around each fillet so it forms a sealed packet.
6. Transfer the parchment packets onto a baking sheet. Bake for 20 minutes.
7. After baking, place a sealed parchment packet on each of the 4 plates and serve hot.

Nutrition:

Nutritional Info (per serving)				
Calories	*Fat*	*Carbs*	*Fiber*	*Protein*
637	43 g	86 g	0 g	80 g

112.   Honey Miso Glazed Salmon

Preparation Time: 5 minutes

Cooking Time: 5 to 10 minutes

Servings: 4

Ingredients:

- 4 salmon fillets
- 2 Tbsp raw honey
- 3 Tbsp miso paste
- 1 tsp coconut aminos
- 1 tsp rice vinegar

Directions:

1. Preheat the broiler.
2. Use aluminum foil to line a baking dish, and add the salmon fillets.
3. Add the honey, miso, coconut aminos and vinegar into a small bowl, stirring them together. Evenly brush over the top of each fillet with the glaze. Broil for about 5 minutes. The fish is done when it flakes easily. Depends on its thickness for the cooking time.
4. Brush over the fish with the remaining glaze and continue to broil for 5 minutes, if needed.

Nutrition:

Nutritional Info (per serving)				
Calories	*Fat*	*Carbs*	*Fiber*	*Protein*
664	29 g	43 g	0 g	60 g

113. Lime Salmon Patties with Dill

Preparation Time: 20 minutes plus 30 minutes chilling

Cooking Time: 10 minutes

Servings: 4

Ingredients:

- 2 Organic eggs
- ½ lb (227 g) cooked boneless salmon fillet, flaked
- 1 scallion, white and green parts, chopped
- ¾ cup almond flour, plus more as needed
- 1 Tbsp chopped fresh dill
- Juice 2 limes (2 to 4 Tbsp), plus more as needed
- Zest 2 limes (optional)
- Pinch sea salt
- 1 Tbsp olive oil
- 1 lime, cut into wedges

Directions:

1. Add the eggs, salmon, scallion, almond flour, dill, lime juice, lime zest (if using) and sea salt into a large bowl, mixing them together until the mixture holds together when pressed. Add more lime juice if it is too dry; add more almond flour if it is too wet.
2. Equally divide the salmon mixture into 4 portions, and press them into about ½-inch thick patties. Transfer them to the refrigerator to chill for about 30 minutes to firm up.
3. Heat the olive oil in a large skillet over medium-high heat.
4. Place the salmon patties into the skillet and brown for about 5 minutes per side, turning once.
5. Serve with lime wedges on the patties.

Nutrition:

Nutritional Info (per serving)				
Calories	*Fat*	*Carbs*	*Fiber*	*Protein*
683	28 g	55 g	0 g	67 g

114.   Tomatoes Stuffed With Tuna and Cheese

Preparation Time: 11 minutes

Cooking Time: 10 minutes

Servings: 2

Ingredients:

- 1 tomato (top cut off and insides scooped)
- 2 tsp balsamic vinegar
- 5 oz canned tuna, drained
- 1 Tbsp mozzarella, chopped
- 1 Tbsp green onion, chopped
- 1 Tbsp basil, chopped

Directions:

1. Take a bowl .
2. Mix the tuna with the vinegar, mozzarella, onion and basil, and stir well.
3. Stuff the tomato with this mix.
4. Serve for lunch.
5. Enjoy!

Nutrition:

Nutritional Info (per serving)				
Calories	*Fat*	*Carbs*	*Fiber*	*Protein*
878	43 g	112 g	16 g	127 g

115. Tuna Salad Mix

Preparation Time: 14 minutes

Cooking Time: 10 minutes

Servings: 4

Ingredients:

- 1 yellow onion, chopped
- ½ cup cilantro, chopped
- 1/3 cup and 2 Tbsp olive oil
- 1 jalapeno pepper, chopped
- 2 Tbsp basil, chopped
- 3 Tbsp white vinegar
- 3 garlic cloves, minced
- 1 tsp red pepper flakes
- 1 tsp thyme, chopped
- A pinch salt and black pepper
- 1 lb sushi tuna, cubed
- 6 oz arugula

Directions:

1. Heat a pan containing about 2 Tbsp of oil over medium-high heat. Then add tuna and season with salt and black pepper.
2. Cook this for 2 minutes on each side before moving to a salad bowl.
3. Add arugula to the mixture and toss well to make sure it is coated.
4. Mix onion with the cilantro, the rest of the oil, jalapeno, basil, vinegar, garlic, pepper flakes, thyme, salt and pepper, and whisk in a clean bowl.
5. Add this to your salad, then toss.
6. Now you can serve.

Nutrition:

Nutritional Info (per serving)				
Calories	*Fat*	*Carbs*	*Fiber*	*Protein*
1689	**46 g**	**211 g**	**11 g**	**216 g**

116.   Tuna with Arugula Sauce

Preparation Time: 15 minutes

Cooking Time: 10 minutes

Servings: 4

Ingredients:

- 3 Tbsp balsamic vinegar
- 1 tsp red pepper flakes
- 1 jalapeño pepper, roughly chopped
- ½ cup fresh cilantro, roughly chopped
- 1 onion, peeled and diced
- ⅓ cup, and 2 Tbsp olive oil
- 2 Tbsp fresh parsley, roughly chopped
- 2 Tbsp fresh basil, roughly chopped

- 1 lb sushi tuna steak
- 2 avocados, pitted, peeled, and sliced
- Salt and black pepper ground, to taste
- A pinch cayenne pepper
- 1 tsp fresh thyme, finely chopped
- 6 oz baby arugula
- 3 garlic cloves, peeled and minced

Directions:

1. Add 1/3 cup of oil to a large bowl along with onion, jalapeno, vinegar, basil, cilantro, parsley, garlic, thyme, pepper flakes, salt, cayenne and black pepper.
2. Mix all of those ingredients well and set the mixture aside.
3. Now pour the remaining oil into a flat pan and let it heat over medium heat.
4. Add the tuna and sear it for 2 minutes per side.
5. Season the tuna with salt and pepper during cooking.
6. Once done, transfer the seared tuna to the cutting board and slice it.
7. Toss arugula with half of the prepared chimichurri mixture in a bowl.
8. Divide this arugula into the serving plates.
9. Top this mixture with tuna slices.
10. Garnish with a drizzle of the remaining chimichurri mixture and avocado slices.

Nutrition:

Nutritional Info (per serving)				
Calories	*Fat*	*Carbs*	*Fiber*	*Protein*
1876	86 g	187 g	12 g	246 g

117.   Potato Salad

Preparation Time: 5 minutes

Cooking Time: 25 minutes

Servings: 4

Ingredients:

- 2 medium potatoes
- 2 medium tomatoes, diced
- 2 celery, diced
- 1 green onion, chopped

Directions:

1. Peel the potatoes. Cut them into cubes, and then place them into a pan.
2. Cook the potatoes for 20 minutes, and when done, drain them and let them cool.
3. Add tomatoes, celery and green onion, season with salt and black pepper, drizzle with oil, and then toss until coated.
4. Divide the salad between 3 bowls and then serve.

Nutrition:

Nutritional Info (per serving)				
Calories	Fat	Carbs	Fiber	Protein
247	9 g	111 g	2.5 g	12 g

118. Super Seed Spelt Pancakes

Preparation Time: 15 minutes

Cooking Time: 10 minutes

Servings: 3

Ingredients:

- 5 oz buckwheat groats
- 1 ½ tsp cinnamon, ground
- 1 ½ oz flax seeds
- 1 ½ oz sesame seeds
- 2 oz chia seeds
- 1 oz pumpkin seeds
- 1 Tbsp almond milk
- ½ tsp stevia extract
- 1 tsp coconut oil
- 1 tsp baking soda
- ½ tsp baking powder
- ¼ tsp fine sea salt

Directions:

1. Grind the pumpkin seeds, sesame seeds, flax seeds, chia seeds and buckwheat groats into flour and keep ¼ of the seed flour for later use (not for this recipe).
2. Add 2 cups of seed flour to a medium bowl.
3. Add in the rest of the ingredients except the coconut oil.
4. Pour in more milk if needed to attain the right consistency.
5. Once heated, pour thin layers of the batter and flip once you see bubbles form on top.
6. Cook until all the batter is used up.

Nutrition:

Nutritional Info (per serving)				
Calories	Fat	Carbs	Fiber	Protein
653	37 g	157 g	12 g	30 g

119.   Scrambled Tofu

Preparation Time: 10 minutes

Cooking Time: 15 minutes

Servings: 2

Ingredients:

- 3 cloves
- 1 onion
- ½ tsp turmeric
- Salt, to taste
- 2 oz firm tofu
- ½ tsp paprika
- 1 handful baby spinach
- 3 tomatoes
- ½ cup yeast
- ½ tsp cumin

Directions:

1. Mince the garlic and dice up the onion.
2. Toss the onions into a pan and let them cook over medium heat for about 7 minutes.
3. Toss in the tofu and tomatoes, and cook for 10 more minutes. Add in some water, cumin and paprika, and stir well. Continue cooking.
4. When the dish is about to cook, add in spinach, stir, and once wilted, turn off the heat and serve.

Nutrition:

Nutritional Info (per serving)				
Calories	*Fat*	*Carbs*	*Fiber*	*Protein*
276	10 g	163 g	0 g	19 g

120.   Tofu Salad

Preparation Time: 10 minutes

Cooking Time: 15 minutes

Servings: 2

Ingredients:

- ½ pack firm tofu
- ¼ Red onion
- 2 spelled tortillas
- 1 avocado
- 4 handfuls baby spinach
- 1 handful almonds
- 2 tomatoes
- 1 pink grapefruit
- ½ lemon

Directions:

1. Bake the tortillas in an oven for 8–10 minutes.
2. Chop up the onions, tomatoes and tofu, and combine this. Put it in the fridge and let it cool.
3. Now chop up the almonds, avocado and grapefruit. Mix everything well and place it in the bowl you had put in the fridge.
4. Squeeze a lemon on top all over the salad and enjoy!

Nutrition:

Nutritional Info (per serving)				
Calories	*Fat*	*Carbs*	*Fiber*	*Protein*
727	12 g	165 g	12 g	46 g

121.   Lentils Chili

Preparation Time: 15 minutes

Cooking Time: 2 hours 6 minutes

Servings: 8

Ingredients:

- 2 tsp olive oil
- 1 large onion, chopped
- 3 medium carrots, peeled and chopped
- 4 celery stalks, chopped
- 2 minced garlic cloves
- 2 Tbsp tomato paste
- 1 ½ Tbsp ground coriander
- 1 ½ Tbsp ground cumin
- 1 ½ tsp ground turmeric
- 1 tsp chipotle chili powder
- Salt and freshly ground black pepper to taste
- 1 lb lentils, rinsed
- 8 cups vegetable broth
- 1 cup fresh spinach, chopped
- ¼ cup fresh mint leaves, chopped
- ¼ cup fresh cilantro, chopped

Directions:

1. In a large pan, heat oil on medium heat.
2. Add onion, carrot and celery, and sauté for about 5 minutes.
3. Add garlic, tomato paste and spices, and sauté for about 1 minute.
4. Add lentils and broth, and bring to a boil.
5. Reduce the heat to low and simmer for about 2 hours.
6. Stir in the spinach and remove from the heat.
7. Serve hot with the garnishing of mint and cilantro.

Nutrition:

Nutritional Info (per serving)				
Calories	*Fat*	*Carbs*	*Fiber*	*Protein*
987	32 g	321 g	0 g	25 g

122.   Easy Slow Cooker Caramelized Onions

Preparation Time: 15 minutes or fewer

Cooking Time: 10 hours on low

Servings: 2 cups

Ingredients:

- 2 Tbsp extra-virgin olive oil
- 4 large onions (white or sweet), sliced very thin
- ½ tsp sea salt

Directions:

1. Add the olive oil, onions and sea salt into the slow cooker, stirring to coat the onions with the oil.
2. Cover the cooker and cook for 10 hours on low. Drain the liquid and serve.

Nutrition:

Nutritional Info (per serving)				
Calories	Fat	Carbs	Fiber	Protein
165	16 g	126 g	0 g	3 g

123.   Quinoa with Veggies

Preparation Time: 15 minutes

Cooking Time: 35 minutes

Servings: 3

Ingredients:

- 2 Tbsp olive oil
- 1 small onion, minced
- 2 carrots, peeled and sliced
- 1 celery stalk, chopped
- 1 garlic clove, minced
- ½ cup uncooked quinoa, rinsed
- 1 tsp ground turmeric
- ¼ tsp dried basil, crushed
- Salt, to taste
- 1 cup vegetable broth
- 1 tsp fresh lime juice

Directions:

1. In a pan, heat oil on medium heat.
2. Add onion, carrot, celery and garlic, and sauté for about t minutes.
3. Stir in the remaining ingredients except for the lime juice and bring to a gentle simmer.
4. Reduce the heat to low and simmer, covered for about 25–30 minutes, or till all the liquid is absorbed.
5. Stir in lime juice and serve.

Nutrition:

Nutritional Info (per serving)				
Calories	Fat	Carbs	Fiber	Protein
457	9 g	211 g	0 g	8 g

124.   Easy Vegetable Stir Fry

Preparation Time: 30 minutes

Cooking Time: 11 minutes

Servings: 4

Ingredients:

- 1 ½ tsp sesame oil
- ¼ cup low-sodium vegetable broth
- 1 Tbsp coconut aminos
- 2 tsp raw honey
- 1 tsp grated fresh ginger
- 1 tsp bottled minced garlic
- 1 tsp arrowroot powder
- 1 cup sliced mushrooms
- 2 carrots, thinly sliced, or about 1 to 1½ cup precut packaged carrots
- 1 celery stalk, thinly sliced on an angle, or ½ cup precut packaged celery
- 2 cups broccoli florets
- 1 cup cauliflower florets
- 1 cup snow peas, halved
- 1 cup bean sprouts
- ¼ cup chopped cashews
- 1 scallion, white and green parts, chopped

Directions:

1. Add the honey, vegetable broth, ginger, coconut aminos, garlic and arrowroot powder in a small bowl, whisking them together until well combined. Set it aside.
2. Add the sesame oil to a large skillet or wok, and heat it over medium-high heat.
3. Stir in the carrots, mushrooms and celery. Sauté for 4 minutes.
4. Add the cauliflower, broccoli and snow peas. Sauté until crisp-tender, about 4 minutes.
5. Stir in the bean sprouts and sauté for 1 minute.
6. Move to one side of the skillet with the vegetables and pour in the sauce. Cook for 2 minutes, stirring until the sauce has thickened. Mix the vegetables into the sauce, and coat well.
7. Top with the cashews and scallion and serve.

Nutrition:

Calories	Fat	Carbs	Fiber	Protein
Nutritional Info (per serving)				
712	16 g	121 g	0 g	73 g

125.   Fresh Spring Roll Wraps

Preparation Time: 20 minutes

Cooking Time: 1 minute

Servings: 4 to 6

Ingredients:

- 2 cups lightly packed baby spinach, divided
- 1 cup grated carrot, divided
- 1 cucumber, halved, seeded, and cut into thin, 4-inch-long strips, divided
- 1 avocado, halved, pitted, and cut into thin strips, divided
- 10 rice paper wrappers

Directions:

1. Find a flat surface to place a cutting board and put the vegetables in front of you.
2. Fill warm water into a large, shallow bowl — hot enough to cook the wrappers, but warm enough so you can touch it comfortably. Soak 1 wrapper in the water and then place it on the cutting board.
3. Fill ¼ cup of spinach, 2 Tbsp of grated carrot, a few cucumber slices and 1 or 2 slices of avocado in the middle of the wrapper.
4. Fold the sides over the middle, and then tightly roll the wrapper from the bottom, burrito-style.
5. Repeat with the remaining wrappers and vegetables.
6. After done, serve immediately.

Nutrition:

Nutritional Info (per serving)				
Calories	*Fat*	*Carbs*	*Fiber*	*Protein*
646	32 g	246 g	0 g	14 g

126. Garlic Mushroom Risotto

Preparation Time: 15 minutes

Cooking Time: 20 minutes

Servings: 4

Ingredients:

- 1 pint sliced mushrooms
- 1 ½ cup Arborio rice
- 2 Tbsp extra-virgin olive oil
- 1 large shallot, sliced
- 1 garlic clove, minced
- 3 cups vegetable broth, warmed
- ½ tsp freshly ground black pepper
- Pinch ground nutmeg
- 1 Tbsp chopped fresh thyme leaves
- 1 tsp salt
- Balsamic vinegar, for garnish

Directions:

1. Add olive oil to a large skillet and heat over high heat. Add the shallot and garlic Sauté for 3 minutes.
2. Stir in the mushrooms and rice. Sauté for another 3 minutes.
3. Lower the heat to medium-high. Add the vegetable broth 1 cup at a time, stirring constantly until the rice has absorbed the liquid before adding another cup of broth.
4. After all the broth is absorbed, add the salt, pepper and nutmeg. Taste the risotto to see if the rice is cooked through; it should be tender but not mushy.
5. Place the risotto in a serving dish. Garnish the thyme leaves over and drizzle with the balsamic vinegar.

Nutrition:

Nutritional Info (per serving)				
Calories	*Fat*	*Carbs*	*Fiber*	*Protein*
983	9 g	160 g	23 g	21 g

127. Mushroom and Pea Buddha Bowl

Preparation Time: 15 minutes

Cooking Time: 35 minutes

Servings: 4–6

Ingredients:

- 3 Tbsp coconut oil (distributed)
- 1 pint sliced mushrooms
- 1 cup brown Arborio rice
- 4 oz (113 g) fresh snow peas, no strings
- 2 carrots, thinly sliced
- ½ cup frozen peas, thawed
- 2 cups vegetable broth
- 2 tsp salt, divided

- 2 garlic cloves, thinly sliced
- 2 scallions, thinly sliced
- Fresh cilantro, chopped at will
- 3 Tbsp lime juice, freshly squeezed
- 1 Tbsp sesame oil, roasted
- 1 Tbsp coconut aminos
- ½ Tbsp red pepper flakes

Directions:

1. In a medium saucepan, combine the Arborio rice, vegetable broth, 1 Tbsp of coconut oil and 1 tsp of salt. Stir well over high heat. Bring to a boil, then reduce to a low heat. Cook for 25 to 35 minutes, or until the rice is cooked, covered in the pot.
2. In a large pan, melt the remaining 2 Tbsp of coconut oil over high heat. Toss in the mushrooms. Cook for 5 minutes, or until gently browned.
3. Add the carrots, snow peas and garlic. Continue to sauté for another 3 minutes. Cover the pan with the thawed peas to keep them heated.
4. Toss the rice with the sautéed vegetables. Add the scallions, cilantro, lime juice, sesame oil, coconut aminos, red pepper flakes and the remaining 1 tsp of salt when ready to serve.

Nutrition:

Nutritional Info (per serving)				
Calories	*Fat*	*Carbs*	*Fiber*	*Protein*
1563	75 g	252 g	0 g	57 g

128.   Grains Chili

Preparation Time: 15 minutes

Cooking Time: 51 minutes

Servings: 8

Ingredients:

- 2 Tbsp olive oil
- 2 shallots, chopped
- 1 large yellow onion, chopped
- 1 Tbsp fresh ginger, grated finely
- 8 garlic cloves, minced
- 1 tsp ground cumin
- 3 Tbsp red chili powder
- Salt and freshly ground black pepper to taste
- (28-oz) can crushed tomatoes
- 1 canned chipotle pepper, minced
- 1 Serrano pepper, seeded and chopped finely
- 2/3 cup bulgur wheat
- 2/3 cup pearl barley
- 2 ¼ cups mixed lentils (green, black, brown), rinsed
- 1 ½ cup canned chickpeas
- 3 scallions, chopped

Directions:

1. In a large pan, heat oil on medium heat.
2. Add shallot and onion, and sauté for about 4–5 minutes.
3. Add ginger, garlic, cumin and chili powder, and sauté for about 1 minute.
4. Stir in tomatoes, both peppers and broth.
5. Stir in the remaining ingredients except for the scallion and bring to a boil.
6. Reduce the heat to low and simmer for about 35–45 minutes or till desired thickness of the chili.
7. Serve hot with the topping of scallion.

Nutrition:

Nutritional Info (per serving)				
Calories	*Fat*	*Carbs*	*Fiber*	*Protein*
1786	123 g	372 g	0 g	112 g

129.   Quinoa and Beans with Veggies

Preparation Time: 20 minutes

Cooking Time: 26 minutes

Servings: 6

Ingredients:

- 2 cups water
- 1 cup dry quinoa
- 2 Tbsp coconut oil
- 1 medium onion, chopped
- 4 garlic cloves, chopped finely
- 2 Tbsp curry powder
- ½ tsp ground turmeric
- Salt, to taste
- 2 cups broccoli, chopped
- 1 cup fresh kale, trimmed and chopped
- 1 cup green peas, shelled
- 1 red bell pepper, seeded and chopped
- 2 cups canned kidney beans, rinsed and drained
- 2 Tbsp fresh lime juice

Directions:

1. In a pan, add water and bring to a boil on high heat.
2. Add quinoa and reduce the heat to low.
3. Simmer for about 10–15 minutes or till all the liquid is absorbed.
4. In a large skillet, melt the coconut oil on a medium heat.
5. Add onion, garlic, curry powder, turmeric and salt, and sauté for about 4–5 minutes.
6. Add the vegetables and cook for about 5–6 minutes.
7. Stir in the quinoa and beans.
8. Drizzle with lime juice and serve.

Nutrition:

Nutritional Info (per serving)				
Calories	Fat	Carbs	Fiber	Protein
1987	54 g	286 g	0 g	62 g

130. Coconut Brown Rice

Preparation Time: 15 minutes

Cooking Time: 1 hour

Servings: 14

Ingredients:

- 12 cups water
- 1 Tbsp dried turmeric
- 2 lb brown rice
- 2 (13½-oz) cans lite coconut milk
- 2 (13½-oz) cans coconut milk
- 1 Tbsp fresh ginger, minced
- 1 ½ tsp fresh lemon zest, grated finely
- 4 dried bay leaves
- Salt and freshly ground black pepper to taste
- Chopped cashews for garnishing
- Chopped fresh cilantro for garnishing

Directions:

1. In a small bowl, add water and turmeric, and beat till well combined.
2. In a large pan, add turmeric, water and the remaining ingredients except for the cashews and stir well.
3. Bring to a boil on high heat.
4. Reduce the heat to medium and simmer, stirring occasionally for about 30–35 minutes.
5. Reduce the heat to low and simmer, covered for about 20–25 minutes.
6. Remove the bay leaf before serving.
7. Garnish with cashews and cilantro, and serve.

Nutrition:

Nutritional Info (per serving)				
Calories	*Fat*	*Carbs*	*Fiber*	*Protein*
2789	126 g	427 g	0 g	198 g

131.   Brown Rice Casserole

Preparation Time: 15 minutes

Cooking Time: 1 hour

Servings: 2

Ingredients:

- 1 tsp extra-virgin olive oil
- 1 red onion, sliced thinly
- 1½ tsp ground turmeric
- 9 oz brown mushrooms, sliced
- 1 tsp raisins
- ½ cup brown rice, rinsed
- 1¼ cup vegetable broth
- ¼ cup fresh cilantro, chopped
- ½ Tbsp pine nuts, toasted
- 1 Tbsp fresh lemon juice
- Salt and freshly ground black pepper, to taste

Directions:

1. Preheat the oven to 400°F.
2. In an ovenproof casserole, heat oil on medium heat.
3. Add onion and turmeric, and sauté for about 3 minutes.
4. Add mushrooms and stir fry for about 2 minutes.
5. Stir in raisins, rice and broth, and transfer into the oven.
6. Bake for about 45–55 minutes or till the desired doneness.
7. Just before serving, stir in the remaining ingredients.

Nutrition:

Nutritional Info (per serving)				
Calories	*Fat*	*Carbs*	*Fiber*	*Protein*
635	15 g	337 g	0 g	15 g

Chapter #8: Desserts and Drinks

132. Green Pudding

Preparation Time: 6 hours and 5 minutes

Cooking Time: 0 minutes

Servings: 4

Ingredients:

- 4 Tbsp coconut milk
- 1 cup coconut cream
- 3 Tbsp hot water
- 4 ½ tsp green tea powder

Directions:

1. In a bowl, mix green tea powder with hot water, stir well, and then cool down.
2. Add milk and cream, stir, and pour into a container.
3. Keep in the freezer for 6 hours before serving frozen.
4. Enjoy!

Nutrition:

Nutritional Info (per serving)				
Calories	*Fat*	*Carbs*	*Fiber*	*Protein*
379	19 g	16 g	5 g	8 g

133.   Green Tea and Chocolate Ice Cream

Preparation Time: 7 hours

Cooking Time: 10 minutes

Servings: 4

Ingredients:

- 2 Tbsp green tea powder
- 1 ½ cup coconut milk
- 1 ½ cup coconut cream
- 2 oz dark chocolate, chopped

Directions:

1. Put the milk in a pan, heat up over medium heat, then add tea powder and cream. Stir, bring to a simmer for a few minutes, then take off the heat and cool down. Keep in the fridge for 3 hours.
2. Transfer the mix to your ice cream maker, add chocolate, then process and freeze according to directions.
3. Freeze for 4 hours more before serving.
4. Enjoy!

Nutrition:

Nutritional Info (per serving)				
Calories	*Fat*	*Carbs*	*Fiber*	*Protein*
453	61 g	198 g	0 g	23 g

134.   Easy Tea Cake

Preparation Time: 10 minutes

Cooking Time: 30 minutes

Servings: 6

Ingredients:

- 6 Tbsp green tea powder
- 2 cups almond milk
- 4 eggs
- 2 tsp vanilla extract
- 3 ½ cup almond flour
- 1 tsp baking soda
- 3 tsp baking powder

Directions:

1. In a bowl, mix the almond milk with green tea powder, eggs, vanilla, almond flour, baking soda and baking powder.
2. Stir until smooth, then pour into a cake pan and place in the oven to bake at 350°F for 30 minutes.
3. Slice and serve cold.
4. Enjoy!

Nutrition:

Nutritional Info (per serving)				
Calories	*Fat*	*Carbs*	*Fiber*	*Protein*
970	59 g	276 g	9 g	65 g

135.   Coconut Cream

Preparation Time: 2 hours

Cooking Time: 5 minutes

Servings: 6

Ingredients:

- 14 oz almond milk
- 14 oz coconut cream
- 1 tsp gelatin powder

Directions:

1. In a pan, mix the almond milk with the cream and gelatin.
2. Stir, bring to a simmer over medium heat, and cook for 5 minutes.
3. Divide into bowls and serve after 2 hours in the fridge.
4. Enjoy!

Nutrition:

Nutritional Info (per serving)				
Calories	*Fat*	*Carbs*	*Fiber*	*Protein*
632	48 g	211 g	3 g	14 g

136.   Pineapple Protein Smoothie

Preparation Time: 5 minutes

Cooking Time: 0 minutes

Servings: 4

Ingredients:

- ½ cup cottage cheese
- ½ cup frozen pineapple
- ½ tsp brown sugar
- ¼ tsp vanilla extract
- 1 Tbsp ground flaxseed
- 1 cup milk choice

Directions:

1. In a blender, combine all the ingredients and stir until smooth.
2. Serve right away.

Nutrition:

Nutritional Info (per serving)				
Calories	*Fat*	*Carbs*	*Fiber*	*Protein*
812	38 g	35 g	38 g	9 g

137.   Pound Cake with Pineapple

Preparation Time: 10 minutes

Cooking Time: 50 minutes

Servings: 8

Ingredients:

- 3 cups all-purpose flour (sifted)
- 2 cups sugar
- 6 whole eggs + 3 egg whites
- 1 tsp vanilla extract
- 1 ½ cup butter
- 1 10-oz can pineapple chunks (rinsed and crushed, keep the juice aside)

For Glaze:

- 1 cup sugar
- 1 stick unsalted butter or margarine
- Reserved juice from the pineapple

Directions:

1. Preheat the oven to 350°F. Beat the sugar and butter until smooth and creamy with a hand mixer. Slowly pour in the eggs (one or two at a time) and whisk thoroughly after each addition. Add the vanilla extract, then the flour, and whisk well.
2. Add the pineapple, which has been drained and diced. Fill a greased cake pan halfway with the batter and bake for 45–50 minutes. Combine the sugar, butter and pineapple juice in a small pot. Bring to a boil, stirring every few seconds. Cook until the glaze has thickened to a creamy consistency. While the cake is still hot, pour the glaze over it. Allow for at least 10 seconds of cooking time before serving.

Nutrition:

Nutritional Info (per serving)				
Calories	*Fat*	*Carbs*	*Sodium*	*Protein*
1369	87 g	278 g	118 mg	92 g

138.   Cashew Cheese Bites

Preparation Time: 5 minutes

Cooking Time: 5 minutes

Servings: 5

Ingredients:

- 8 oz cream cheese
- 1 tsp cinnamon
- 1 cup cashew butter

Directions:

1. In a blender, combine all the ingredients and mix until smooth.
2. Fill the small muffin liners halfway with the combined mixture and chill until firm.
3. Serve and have fun.

Nutrition:

Nutritional Info (per serving)				
Calories	*Fat*	*Carbs*	*Sodium*	*Protein*
547	29 g	15 g	75 mg	5 g

139.   Energy Booster Sunflower Balls

Preparation Time: 10 minutes

Cooking Time: 10 minutes

Servings: 25

Ingredients:

- 1 cup sunflower seeds
- 2 oz unsweetened chocolate (melted)
- 1 Tbsp water
- 8 drops liquid Stevia

Directions:

1. Blend the sunflower seeds until finely pulverized in a blender.
2. Blend in the water, Stevia, and melted chocolate until a firm dough-like substance forms.
3. Form little balls out of the batter and set them on a baking sheet. Refrigerate for 30 minutes before serving.
4. Serve and have fun!

Nutrition:

Nutritional Info (per serving)				
Calories	Fat	Carbs	Sodium	Protein
563	12 g	63 g	65 mg	5 g

140.   Peach Cobbler

Preparation Time: 5 minutes

Cooking Time: 25 minutes

Servings: 6

Ingredients:

- ¼ cup coconut palm sugar, divided
- 2 peaches, chopped
- ¾ cup pecans, chopped
- ½ tsp cinnamon
- ½ cup oats, gluten-free
- ¼ cup (brown) rice flour
- ¼ cup flaxseeds, ground
- ¼ cup olive oil, extra-virgin

Directions:

1. Set the oven temperature to 350°F.
2. Grease the bottom of 6 ramekins.
3. In a mixing bowl, combine the peaches, cinnamon, ½ Tbsp of coconut sugar and pecans.
4. The peach mixture should be placed halfway up the ramekins.
5. Oats, rice flour, flaxseed, and oil should all be combined in the same bowl. The residual vanilla extract and the coconut sugar should be combined in a different bowl. Mix until the mixture resembles crumbles.
6. Place the mix at 350°F in the oven for 20 minutes.

Nutrition:

Nutritional Info (per serving)				
Calories	*Fat*	*Carbs*	*Fiber*	*Protein*
898	**25 g**	**72 g**	**0 g**	**16 g**

141.   Sweet Ginger Bread Loaf

Preparation Time: 20 minutes

Cooking Time: 1 hour

Servings: 16

Ingredients:

- Unsalted butter (for greasing the baking dish)
- 3 cups all-purpose flour
- 1 large egg
- ½ tsp baking soda substitute
- 2 tsp ground cinnamon
- 1 tsp ground allspice
- ¾ cup granulated sugar
- ¼ cup olive oil
- 2 Tbsp molasses
- 1¼ cup plain rice milk
- 2 tsp grated fresh ginger
- Powdered sugar (for dusting)

Directions:

1. Preheat the oven to 350°F.
2. Set aside a 9-by-13-inch baking dish that has been lightly greased with butter. Sift together the flour, baking soda replacement, cinnamon and allspice in a large mixing bowl. In a separate bowl, combine the flour and sugar.
3. Whisk the milk, egg, olive oil, molasses and ginger in a medium mixing bowl until thoroughly combined. Make a well in the middle of the flour mixture and pour in the wet ingredients. Mix just until everything is incorporated, being careful not to overmix.
4. Fill the baking dish halfway with batter and bake for 1 hour, or until a wooden pick inserted in the center comes out clean.
5. Serve warm with a coating of powdered sugar.

Nutrition:

Nutritional Info (per serving)				
Calories	*Fat*	*Carbs*	*Sodium*	*Protein*
1467	56 g	162 g	18 mg	34 g

142. Chocolate Almond Custard

Preparation Time: 10 minutes

Cooking Time: 15 minutes

Servings: 3

Ingredients:

- 3 chocolate cookies, chunks
- A pinch salt
- ¼ tsp cardamom, ground
- 3 Tbsp honey
- ¼ tsp nutmeg, freshly grated

- 2 Tbsp butter
- 3 Tbsp whole milk
- 1 cup almond flour
- 3 eggs
- 1 tsp pure vanilla extract

Directions:

1. In a mixing bowl, beat the eggs with butter. Now, add the milk and continue mixing until well combined.
2. Add the remaining ingredients in the order listed above. Divide the batter among 3 ramekins.
3. Add 1 cup of water and a metal trivet to the Instant Pot.
4. Cover the ramekins with foil and lower them onto the trivet.
5. Secure the lid and select Manual mode.
6. Cook at high pressure for 12 minutes. Once cooking is complete, use a quick release; carefully remove the lid.
7. Transfer the ramekins to a wire rack and allow them to cool slightly before serving.
8. Enjoy!

Nutrition:

Calories	Fat	Carbs	Sugar	Protein
1246	35 g	82 g	21.1 g	60 g

143.   Buttery Pound Cake

Preparation Time: 20 minutes

Cooking Time: 1 hour 15 minutes

Servings: 20

Ingredients:

- Unsalted butter (for greasing the baking pan)
- All-purpose flour (for dusting the baking pan)
- 2 cups unsalted butter (at room temperature)
- 3 cups granulated sugar
- 6 eggs (at room temperature)
- 1 Tbsp pure vanilla extract
- 4 cups all-purpose flour
- ¾ cup unsweetened rice milk

Directions:

1. Preheat the oven to 325°F.
2. Set aside a 10-inch Bundt pan that has been greased with butter and dusted with flour. Hand-mix the butter and sugar in a large mixing basin for approximately 4 minutes, or until extremely frothy and pale.
3. One at a time, beat in the eggs, scraping down the sides of the basin after each addition. Blend in the vanilla extract. Alternate the flour and rice milk in 3 additions, with the flour coming in first and last.
4. Fill the Bundt pan halfway with batter. Bake for 1 hour and 15 minutes, or until the cake's top is golden brown and springs back when softly pushed. Cool the cake in the Bundt pan for 10 minutes on a wire rack.
5. Before serving, remove the cake from the pan and cool fully on a wire rack.

Nutrition:

Nutritional Info (per serving)				
Calories	*Fat*	*Carbs*	*Sodium*	*Protein*
1119	99 g	489 g	28 mg	16 g

144.   Pumpkin Cheesecake Bar

Preparation Time: 10 minutes

Cooking Time: 50 minutes

Servings: 4

Ingredients:

- 1 ½ Tbsp butter
- 2 egg white
- ½ cup all-purpose white flour
- 3 Tbsp golden brown sugar
- ¼ cup granulated sugar
- 4 oz cream cheese
- 1 tsp ground nutmeg
- ½ cup pureed pumpkin
- 1 tsp ground cinnamon
- 1 tsp vanilla extract

Directions:

1. Preheat the oven to 350°F/170°C/Gas Mark 4.
2. Take the butter and cream cheese out of the refrigerator. In a mixing dish, combine the flour and brown sugar. To make 'breadcrumbs,' rub in the butter with your fingers. ¾ of this mixture should go into the bottom of an oven-safe dish. Remove from the oven after 15 minutes to cool.
3. Whisk the egg lightly, then mix the cream cheese, sugar (or stevia), pumpkin, cinnamon, nutmeg and vanilla until creamy.
4. Pour this mixture over the cooked foundation and top with the remainder of the breadcrumbs you set up earlier. Return to the oven for another 30–35 minutes of baking.
5. Allow cooling before slicing.

Nutrition:

Nutritional Info (per serving)				
Calories	*Fat*	*Carbs*	*Sodium*	*Protein*
621	23 g	73 g	146 mg	11 g

145.   Lemon Delight

Preparation Time: 10 minutes

Cooking Time: 30 minutes

Servings: 2

Ingredients:

- 1 Tbsp Polyunsaturated margarine
- 1 Egg
- ¼ cup Caster sugar
- ¼ cup Self-rising flour
- ½ cup water
- 1 small lemon (zest + juice)

Directions:

1. Cream the margarine, sugar, egg yolk, water and flour until smooth in a mixing dish. Gently fold the egg whites into the batter mixture using a metal spoon until firm.
2. Pour into a greased ovenproof dish and bake for 20–30 minutes, or until golden brown on top, at 350°F (Gas Mark 4).
3. Serve warm with a sprinkling of caster sugar.

Nutrition:

Nutritional Info (per serving)				
Calories	*Fat*	*Carbs*	*Sodium*	*Protein*
567	18 g	67 g	7 mg	6 g

146. Mocha Cherry Smoothie

Preparation Time: 10 minutes

Cooking Time: 0 minutes

Servings: 2

Ingredients:

- 1 cup (unsweetened) chocolate almond milk
- 1 cup (unsweetened) cherries, frozen and pitted
- 6 oz vanilla Greek yogurt, fat-free
- 2 Tbsp cocoa powder, unsweetened
- ½ banana, medium
- 2 Tbsp almond butter
- 1 tsp vanilla
- 1 tsp powdered espresso coffee, instant
- 2 cups ice cubes
- 1 Tbsp (chocolate-covered) espresso beans, dark chocolate shavings

Directions:

1. Cherries, almond milk, almond butter, Greek yogurt, banana, espresso coffee powder, cocoa powder and vanilla all go into a blender.
2. Blend under cover until smooth. Ice cubes should be added; cover and blend till smooth. Pour into glasses and, if you like, top with more banana slices, chocolate-covered espresso beans, or both.

Nutrition:

Nutritional Info (per serving)				
Calories	Fat	Carbs	Fiber	Protein
472	12 g	34 g	0 g	19 g

147.   Strawberry Smoothie

Preparation Time: 10 minutes

Cooking Time: 0 minutes

Servings: 2

Ingredients:

- 1 cup strawberries
- 1 ½ cup milk
- 1 large banana
- 2 Tbsp almonds

Directions:

1. In a high-speed mixing blender, add all the ingredients and pulse until smooth.
2. Transfer into 2 serving glasses and serve immediately.

Nutrition:

Nutritional Info (per serving)				
Calories	*Fat*	*Carbs*	*Sodium*	*Protein*
427	3 g	67 g	45 mg	19 g

148. Apple and Pear Smoothie

Preparation Time: 10 minutes

Cooking Time: 0 minutes

Servings: 2

Ingredients:

- 2 green apples
- 2 cups fresh mustard greens
- ¼ cup ice cubes
- 2 pears
- ¼ tsp cinnamon
- 1 ½ cup filtered water

Directions:

1. In a high-speed mixing blender, add all the ingredients and pulse until smooth.
2. Transfer into two serving glasses and serve immediately.

Nutrition:

Calories	Fat	Carbs	Sodium	Protein
165	3 g	73 g	3 mg	2.9 g

149.   Cherry Drink

Preparation Time: 5 minutes

Cooking Time: 0 minutes

Servings: 4

Ingredients:

- 2 cups cherries
- 5 cups water
- 1 Tbsp honey

Directions:

1. Bring to a boil the mixture of water and cherries.
2. Drink into glasses, then top with liquid honey.

Nutrition:

Nutritional Info (per serving)				
Calories	*Fat*	*Carbs*	*Fiber*	*Protein*
157	2 g	36 g	0 g	2 g

150. Coconut Late

Preparation Time: 5 minutes

Cooking Time: 10 minutes

Servings: 4

Ingredients:

- 4 tsp coffee, ground
- 1 Tbsp coconut, shredded
- 2 cups coconut milk
- 1 cup water

Directions:

1. Turn on the heat and get the water boiling.
2. Stir in the ground coffee.
3. Pour the liquid into the glasses.
4. Add coconut shavings and coconut milk.

Nutrition:

Nutritional Info (per serving)				
Calories	Fat	Carbs	Fiber	Protein
489	48 g	19 g	0 g	5 g

151. Avocado Grape Smoothie

Preparation Time: 10 minutes

Cooking Time: 0 minutes

Servings: 1

Ingredients:

- 1 pear, chopped
- 1 Tbsp lime juice, fresh
- 6 oz Greek yogurt, plain
- 1 Tbsp avocado
- 15 pieces (red/green) grapes
- ½ cup spinach leaves, packed

Directions:

1. To a blender, add all the ingredients.
2. Blend until creamy and smooth.
3. Offer and savor.

Nutrition:

Nutritional Info (per serving)				
Calories	Fat	Carbs	Fiber	Protein
555	23 g	57 g	0 g	23 g

Chapter #9: 30-Days Meal Plan with Conversion Chart and Shopping List

Shopping List for an Anti-Inflammatory Diet

Poultry, Meat and Seafood, and Eggs

- Whole Chicken
- Chicken Breasts
- Chicken Thighs
- Lean Ground Turkey
- Cooked Duck
- Sirloin Steak
- Flank Steak
- Cooked Beef Meat
- Lean Ground Beef
- Pork Tenderloin
- Pork Chops
- Boneless Lamb
- Lamb Necks
- Lean Ground Lamb
- Salmon
- Halibut
- Cod
- Tilapia
- Sea Bass
- Snapper
- Shrimp
- Prawns
- Scallops
- Eggs
- Lamb
- Herring
- Sardines
- Mackerel
- Wild Salmon
- Grass-Fed Beef, Bison
- Chicken Breasts, Chicken Thighs

Veggies

- Okra
- Beets
- Yams
- Leeks
- Garlic
- Fennel
- Jicama
- Chives
- Celery
- Endive
- Carrots
- Onions
- Escarole

- Chicory
- Broccoli
- Shallots
- Sprouts
- Turnips
- Spinach
- Parsnips
- Radishes
- Romaine
- Scallions
- Rhubarb
- Arugula
- Zucchini
- Pumpkin
- Radicchio
- Avocados
- Rutabagas
- Asparagus
- Tomatoes
- Tomatillos
- Watercress
- Cucumbers
- Radish leaves
- Turnip greens
- Sweet potatoes
- Collard greens
- Kale (all types)
- Mustard greens
- Brussels sprouts
- Daikon radishes

- Chinese cabbage
- Dandelion greens
- Lettuce (all types)
- Chard, (all variants)
- Broccoli rabe (rapini)
- Olives (fresh, not canned)
- Cabbage (red and green variants)
- Tobacco peppers (any variant or color)
- Vegetables native to Asia, including bok choy
- Sea veggies (nori, kombu, dulse, kelp, and wakame)
- Squash (all variants including winter and summer varieties)

Fruits

- Kiwi
- Pears
- Dates
- Plums
- Limes
- Lemons
- Mangoes
- Oranges
- Prunes
- Guava
- Grapes
- Apples
- Peaches
- Papayas

- Raisins
- Bananas
- Apricots
- Coconut
- Cherries
- Currants
- Nectarines
- Grapefruit
- Goji berries
- Figs (fresh)
- Muskmelon
- Blueberries
- Blackberries
- Cantaloupes
- Cranberries
- Persimmons
- Pineapples
- Tangerines
- Watermelon
- Raspberries
- Strawberries
- Pomegranates
- Honeydew melon
- Dried fruit (sulfur/ no added sugar/ additives)

Condiments

- Salsa
- Cocoa
- Sea salt

- Olive oil
- Hummus
- Mustard
- Guacamole
- Apple cider vinegar
- Balsamic vinegar
- Dairy-Free Milk
- Hemp milk
- Almond milk
- Cashew milk
- Coconut milk
- Culinary coconut milk
- Oat milk (from gluten-free oats)

Beverages

- Herbal teas
- Pure water
- Pure water
- Coconut milk
- Grass-fed whey protein
- Vegetable juices
- Almond milk (without sugar)
- Gluten-Free Baking Flours
- Almond flour
- Coconut flour
- Almond meal
- Gluten-free oat flour
- Chickpea flour (garbanzo bean)

Sweeteners

- Stevia
- Honey (raw)
- Coconut sugar
- Dark chocolate

Supplements

- Spirulina
- Resveratrol
- Ginger extract
- Fish oil extract

- Curcumin extract
- Alpha-Lipoic Acid

Seeds and Nuts

- Almonds
- Chia seeds
- Nuts from Brazil
- Ground flaxseed
- Cashews
- Hemp seeds
- Hazelnuts
- Nut macadamia
- Brazil, almond, cashew, pumpkin, pecan, walnut, and sunflower butter
- Pine nuts
- Pecans

- Sesame seeds
- Pumpkin seeds
- Paste of tahini
- Sunflower seeds
- Walnuts

Spices and Herbs

- Pepper ancho
- Bay leaves
- Basil
- Cardamom
- Freshly ground black pepper
- Seeds from celery
- Pepper cayenne
- Powdered chili
- Chervil
- Powdered chipotle
- Red chilies
- Cinnamon, ground or sticks
- Coriander cilantro (ground)
- Cumin
- Cloves
- Curry powder with dill
- Powdered five-spice
- Fennel seeds
- Fresh garlic
- Masala garam
- Gomasio

- Fresh and ground ginger
- Marjoram
- Lemongrass
- Powdered mustard
- Mint
- Mustard seeds
- Oregano
- Nutmeg
- Parsley
- Paprika
- Red pepper flakes (crushed)
- Turmeric
- Rosemary
- Black peppercorns
- Saffron
- Sage
- Anise star
- Sea salt
- Thyme
- Tarragon

Legumes and Beans

- Garbanzo beans/chickpeas
- Green and brown lentils
- Peas (snow, green, and sugar snap)

Extra:

- Olive oil
- Coconut oil
- Sesame oil
- MCT oil
- Olive oil cooking spray
- Almond meal
- Almond flour
- Coconut flour
- Chickpea flour
- Arrowroot flour
- Arrowroot powder
- Arrowroot starch
- Baking powder
- Baking soda
- Protein powder
- Matcha green tea powder
- Cacao powder
- Dijon mustard
- Nutritional yeast
- Apple cider vinegar
- Vanilla extract
- Coconut aminos
- Fish sauce
- Coconut sugar
- Stevia
- Organic honey
- Maple syrup
- Almond butter
- Sugar-free pumpkin puree
- Unsweetened dried cranberries
- Unsweetened coconut
- Chicken broth
- Beef broth
- Vegetable broth

30-Days Meal Plan

DAYS	BREAKFAST	LUNCH	DINNER	DESSERTS
1	Zucchini muffins	Mushroom and Pea Buddha Bowl	Grains Chili	Lemon Delight
2	Spiced Oatmeal	Shrimp Fried Rice	Homemade Garlic Confit with Herb	Green Pudding
3	Quinoa and Pumpkin Porridge	Fresh Spring Roll Wraps	Garlic Mushroom Risotto	Green Tea and Chocolate Ice Cream
4	Banana Pancakes	Easy Vegetable Stir Fry	Quinoa with Veggies	Mocha Cherry Smoothie
5	Cauliflower and Kale Bowl with Avocado	Easy Slow Cooker Caramelized Onions	Lentils Chili	Easy Tea Cake
6	Chia Seed Pudding with Berries on Top	Scrambled Tofu	Tofu Salad	Avocado Grape Smoothie
7	Chickpea Fritters	Potato Salad	Zucchini Pepper Chips	Pineapple Protein Smoothie

DAYS	BREAKFAST	LUNCH	DINNER	DESSERTS
8	Quinoa and Pumpkin Porridge	Spicy Salmon Fillets with Salad	Roasted Salmon with Herb Gremolata	Coconut Cream
9	Blueberry Banana Baked Oatmeal	Salmon and Kale in Parchment	Salmon Burgers	Pound Cake with Pineapple
10	Banana Steel Cut Walnut Oats	Oven-Fried Fish with Pineapple Salsa	White Fish and Broccoli Curry	Cashew Cheese Bites
11	Spinach and Artichoke Egg Casserole	Shrimp Fried Rice	Creamy Shrimp Fettuccine	Energy Booster Sunflower Balls
12	Coconut Almond Granola	Shrimp Skewers with Mango Cucumber Salsa	Shrimp and Bok Choy in Parchment	Peach Cobbler
13	Easy Coconut Pancakes	Smoked Salmon with Eggs Salad	Baked Salmon with Pea and Broccoli Mash	Sweet Ginger Bread Loaf
14	Easy Overnight Oats	Mussels with Creamy Tarragon Sauce	Thai Curry with Prawns	Chocolate Almond Custard

DAYS	BREAKFAST	LUNCH	DINNER	DESSERTS
15	Carrots Breakfast Mix	Wrapped Salmon	Sesame Salmon with Broccoli and Tomatoes	Buttery Pound Cake
16	Italian Breakfast Salad	Salmon and Salsa	Shrimp fajita	Pumpkin Cheesecake Bar
17	Zucchini and Sprout Breakfast Mix	Simple Sardines and Cucumber Mix	Steak Tuna	Lemon Delight
18	Breakfast Corn Salad	Simple Baked Catfish with Salad	Shrimp and Calamari with Avocado Sauce	Mocha Cherry Smoothie
19	Cilantro pancakes	Seared beef soup bowls	Seared beef with peanut sauce	Pound Cake with Pineapple
20	Zucchini muffins	Sauerkraut Soup and Beef	Rosemary lamb bowls	Cherry Drink
21	Breakfast Omelet	Spicy Grainy Lamb	Roasted Beef and pepperoncini	Coconut Late

DAYS	BREAKFAST	LUNCH	DINNER	DESSERTS
22	Breakfast Avocado Boat	Perfect Pulled Pork	Lamb and Ginger Stir Fry	Avocado Grape Smoothie
23	Breakfast Casserole	Pork Salad	Easy Pork Chops	Peach Cobbler
24	Sweet Potato Hash	Sweet and Sour Pork	Healthy Mushroom and Olive Sirloin Steak	Baked Zucchini
25	Breakfast Avocado Boat	Spicy Paprika Lamb Chops	Lamb Chops with Redcurrant and Mint Sauce	Roast green beans with cranberries
26	Breakfast Strata	Beef Stew	Pork Rolls	Roasted cheesy mushrooms
27	Amaranth Porridge with Pears	Pan-seared sausage and kale	Nutmeg Meatballs Curry	Sweets With Carrots And Chocolate
28	Sweet Potato Breakfast Bowl	Pork Meatballs	Chuck Roast and Veggies	Chestnut Panini With Fennels
29	Strawberry Smoothie	Beef and Vegetable Soup	Tarragon Pork Steak	Lime Cilantro Rice
30	Italian Breakfast Salad	Pork and Creamy Veggie Sauce	Ground Pork Pan	Spicy Mushroom Stir Fry

Measurement Conversion Chart

VOLUME EQUIVALENTS(DRY)

US STANDARD	METRIC (APPROXIMATE)
1/8 teaspoon	0.5 mL
1/4 teaspoon	1 mL
1/2 teaspoon	2 mL
3/4 teaspoon	4 mL
1 teaspoon	5 mL
1 tablespoon	15 mL
1/4 cup	59 mL
1/2 cup	118 mL
3/4 cup	177 mL
1 cup	235 mL
2 cups	475 mL
3 cups	700 mL
4 cups	1 L

VOLUME EQUIVALENTS(LIQUID)

US STANDARD	US STANDARD (OUNCES)	METRIC (APPROXIMATE)
2 tablespoons	1 fl.oz.	30 mL
1/4 cup	2 fl.oz.	60 mL
1/2 cup	4 fl.oz.	120 mL
1 cup	8 fl.oz.	240 mL
1 1/2 cup	12 fl.oz.	355 mL
2 cups or 1 pint	16 fl.oz.	475 mL
4 cups or 1 quart	32 fl.oz.	1 L
1 gallon	128 fl.oz.	4 L

TEMPERATURES EQUIVALENTS

FAHRENHEIT(F)	CELSIUS(C) (APPROXIMATE)
225 °F	107 °C
250 °F	120 °C
275 °F	135 °C
300 °F	150 °C
325 °F	160 °C
350 °F	180 °C
375 °F	190 °C
400 °F	205 °C
425 °F	220 °C
450 °F	235 °C
475 °F	245 °C
500 °F	260 °C

WEIGHT EQUIVALENTS

US STANDARD	METRIC (APPROXIMATE)
1 ounce	28 g
2 ounces	57 g
5 ounces	142 g
10 ounces	284 g
15 ounces	425 g
16 ounces (1 pound)	455 g
1.5 pounds	680 g
2 pounds	907 g

Conclusion

Thank you for reading this anti-inflammatory cookbook. When making any type of lifestyle change, it is critical to have a plan. Not having a plan, especially when it comes to food, can leave you disappointed and broke. Changing your diet affects many aspects of your life.

If you do not live alone, you must also take into account your family's nutritional needs, preferences, allergies, finances, and time availability. You'll also need to decide which foods to include in your anti-inflammatory diet and which to avoid. By combining all of this information, you can effectively create a strategy that clears your path to lower inflammation.

The key is to eliminate foods that cause inflammation, which aids in the healing of your gut and immune system.

It makes no difference if you have a history of chronic inflammation; eating in an anti-inflammatory manner is always a good idea. Eating to reduce inflammation is more than a fad; it's a lifestyle choice that will improve your well-being, health, and overall quality of life in the long run. A diet like this benefits everyone, but in my experience, it is especially beneficial for those who are dealing with chronic health issues and inflammation.

If you have a health problem, don't expect immediate results; depending on the circumstances, it could take up to a month and a half to see long-term or short-term benefits.

Good luck.

Recipe Index

😃 THERE IS A SURPRISE FOR YOU 😃

🎁 <u>A GIFT FOR YOU</u> 🎁

<u>Scan Now</u>

What Will You Receive Scanning Above?

✔️ A comprehensive Look at the science of your Healthy Eating and its impact on your Body.
✔️ A debunk of Myths, providing a Balanced view backed by scientific evidence.
✔️ A step-by-step Guide to making sustainable changes

...And a your rating is very appreciated. Thank you!!

https://www.amazon.com/review/create-review?&ASIN=B0C6VZ234P

Olivia Jane Fisher

StayHealthy

Contact us misterbondwriter@gmail.com or Scan Here
For more Info about Physical and Mental Well-Being

Made in the USA
Middletown, DE
18 January 2024

48104881R00104